THE BOUNDARY OF BLUR

THE BOUNDARY OF BLUR

Nick Piombino

ROOF BOOKS • NEW YORK

Cover drawing by Toni Simon.
Design by Deborah Thomas.

ISBN: 0-937804-50-9
Library of Congress Catalog Card No.: 92-63355

This book was made possible, in part, by a grant from the New York State
Council on the Arts.

Roof Books
are published by
Segue Foundation
303 East 8th Street
New York, New York 10009

for Toni Simon

Let us define the limits. There are no boundaries in things. Laws try to impose some, and the mind cannot bear it.

Blaise Pascal

ACKNOWLEDGMENTS

In *L=A=N=G=U=A=G=E*: "Writing and Free Association" (Feb. 1978, Vol. 1, no. 1); "Writing and Self-Disclosure" (June 1978, No. 3); "Writing as Reverie" (Oct. 1978, No. 5); "Writing and Remembering" (March 1979, No. 7); "Writing and Imaging" (June 1979, No. 8); "Writing and Experiencing" (Jan. 1979, No. 11); "Writing and Conceiving" (Dec. 1980, No. 13)

"The Talismanic Value of Words in Private Thought" in *A Critical Ninth Assembling, 1979*

"Writing, Identity and the Self" in *The Difficulties, 1982*

"The Indeterminate Interval: From History to Blur" (with Alan Davies, in *L=A=N=G=U=A=G=E* (Vol. 4) issue of *Open Letter*, 1982, Fifth Series, No. 1)

"Writing as Reverie," "Writing and Experiencing," and "Writing and Imaging" in *The L=A=N=G=U=A=G=E Book*, Southern Illinois University Press, 1984

"Towards An Experiential Syntax" in *Poetics Journal*, No. 5, May 1985

"Language as Actuality" was presented at the symposium "Beyond Words and Phrases"at the Zen Community of New York Graystone Seminary,1985

"Subject to Change" was presented at "Subject Matter: A Forum" at The Poetry Project, NY, 1985, and at Intersection in San Francisco on 1986

"Writing and Conceiving" in *In The American Tree*, National Poetry Foundation,1986

"Subject to Change" and "Currents of Attention in the Poetic Process" in *Temblor 5*, 1987

"9/8/86 - 12/29/87" in *Project Papers* (Vol. 1, No. 21, The Poetry Project, NY, 1988

"Aftermath: 1/1/88 - 2/13/88" in *Temblor 9*, 1989

"9/4/88" in PATTERNS/CONTEXT/TIME A Symposium on Contemporary Poetry, *Tyuonyi*, 1990

"9/20/88 - 9/2/89" in *Verse*, Vol. 7, No. 1, Spring 1990

"Aftermath: Epilogue to the Boundary of Blur (9/8/86 - 12/29/87)" in *Avec*, Fourth Issue, 1990

"Writing and Spontaneity" and "Writing and Persevering" were first presented as a talk at the State University at Buffalo, 1990.

"Writing and Spontaneity" in *The Poetry Project Newsletter*, 1991

"Writing and Persevering" in *Witz*, 1992

"Cultivate Your Own Wilderness" in *The Politics of Poetic Form*, 1990

"Writing and Spontaneity" and "Writing and Persevering" in a chapbook (Leave Books, Buffalo)

The author wishes to extend grateful acknowledgement to the editors of the above publications for their efforts on behalf of his work: Bruce Andrews, Tom Beckett, Charles Bernstein, Cydney Chadwick, Phillip Foss, Ed Friedman, Lyn Hejinian, the late Leland Hickman, Richard Kostelanetz, Jerome McGann, Christopher Reiner, Jerome Sala, Ron Silliman, Juliana Spahr, Barrett Watten.

CONTENTS

WRITING AND FREE ASSOCIATION

The method of self-disclosure called "free association," wherein one writes or speaks all one's thoughts in consecutive order (also sometimes called "automatic writing" in literary criticism), is comparable to serious attempts to read, write, and understand poetry that direct attention to the totality of the thinking process. Memories and awareness of the present collapse into an experiential field composed of verbal presences that can be re-sounded for various interpretations and alternative directions. Both in writing poetry and in free association one frequently listens for meanings rather than just directing the thought process in a purposive way to get to them.

When poets choose the moments they will inscribe on the page the lettered representations of what they wish to present to be read, they become the creators of their own reading. As they reread they can experience the moments they chose to move from the position of listeners to that of recorders. These signs they make to reread are the hieroglyphic constructs by which they hope to disclose the experiential process simultaneous to the poem's conception. Not that the line or the poem is merely a "slice of thought" corresponding to the naturalistic construct of a stage upon which the writer reenacts a narrative representation of a conception of an experience. The very choice of moments for writing poetry is part of the mysterious flow of attention alert in the mind of poets to the tides and currents of their own perceptions. By means of their poems they attempt to catch their thoughts in their nascent state, malleable, yet in such a way that their original sense may be maintained. When they abandon the possibility of authenticity, celebrate the inevitability of masks and roles, "play the game," or imitate what they imagine would be successful, they are resting from or resisting the more difficult work of finding clues to the solutions the unconscious keeps presenting in various kinds of puzzles and disguises. Aware of the silence that ever more deeply underlines their utterances, drawn on by the music represented by these letters from the unconscious, by a kind of retrograde movement of language, they are led closer to the other voices of the self. Finding ways of noticing these thoughts at the moments of their inner presentation, they may isolate momentarily what is ordinarily most immediate to experience but otherwise most elusive. When we read poems we simultaneously listen to our personal associations as well as the intended meanings of words. "Words are notes on the keyboard of the imagination." (Wittgenstein) And Freud: "It is only too easy to forget that a dream is a thought like any other." Like the sequential motifs in dreams, a poem's meaning often appears to be more verbal than literal, resonating with meaning rather than describing it. Sometimes sequences in poems (and in dreams and thoughts) can be drawn together like fragments in a collage, to open another implied area not yet found. What is before can become what is next (to). For example, in writing poetry the very next thought may seem technically unacceptable, but allowed to remain in the poem it may later reveal an otherwise hidden intention.

In psychoanalysis attempts toward free association reveal to the analysand emotions that underlie everyday conflicts. These verbalizations are interpreted by the analyst and the analysand with the goal of increasing the analysand's awareness of alternatives. There are parallels between such experiences and the complex relationship that arises between the poet and the poem. While the poet observes and directs the thought process, experiences of subjective and objective comprehension fuse and alternate, accelerating the mind towards associations of various types of meanings, intensities, and emotions. Language demands to be said, heard, felt, and comprehended all at once, out of the sphere of choosing actions, as the poet is immersed in the consciousness of the poem's tremors, intentions, and implications. Like the poem, the free associative process goes from segment to segment with a continual sense of arbitrariness and complete choice.

later the reader is immersed in the poem's consciousness as well

all ... immersed = collective conscious...

WRITING AND SELF-DISCLOSURE

With the publication of *The Interpretation of Dreams* (1900), Freud reframed and refined an enigma that haunts most literary efforts to combine a revelation of self and other: can, and, if it can, how does this aspect of literature help anyone else? He showed that by analyzing his own dreams by means of an associative method of interpretation he could heal his own neurosis. In a uniquely psychological fashion Freud succeeded in convincing many members of his own generation of contemplative readers, and many of those in succeeding generations, of the value of self-reflection. By transposing his findings into a viable mode of intersubjective discourse, he proposed a vehicle found in practice to release previously inhibited psychic energies. Like an artist, an analysand with the help of the analyst, by disclosing inner psychic processes, would connect with the core of his or her being and by completing this circuit, reintegrate his or her personality.

Just as the Senoi Indians discovered and exploited group reveries in their own group,[1] Freud found that efforts to probe the unconscious may have distinctly healing effects. Like the shaman, the poet experiences the healing power of the act of writing through the reading and rereading of texts. Now, with parallel concerns, the psychoanalytic theorist (c.f. the work of D.W. Winnicott) can return to the group the labyrinth of common self-deceptions concealed in unconscious mental processes.

For poets, and readers of poetry, a technique of sharing dreams is readily available: the exchange of texts. These texts are revelations of a poet's direct encounter with the process of creating a language structured in a way commensurate with a personal need to articulate perceptions. The mapping of this path for the contemporary poet is often dotted with islands or cities of personal disclosure — over and over he names himself, because it is through this successive identification of selves that he literally knows where he is. The other is no longer brother or sister or son or daughter, another symbol of another herald, but simply the legend of another map of the same terrain.

The boldest of contemporary poets are often the least shy about revealing themselves. What saves, for example, John Ashbery's poetry from its own formalism is its readiness to blurt out its author's human vulnerabilities. Whether his lines or sentences are fragmentary (as in *The Tennis Court Oath*) or sustained and elaborated (as in *Three Poems*), I feel the presence of a willingness, even if it might sometimes appear unexpected, or arbitrary, to share his humanness with me. This is what I hear in what others might describe as "obscure personal associations." He confronts the possibility of a voluntary withdrawal on the part of his reader because of embarrassment or confusion. We see ourselves in this because we know that we have also consented to turn away at times from the painful clarity of identifying, for example, certain kinds of access to hidden truths about ourselves.

Contemporary poets discover their formal matrices through a process of self-disclosure that is contiguous with their creations. This process reveals to them the form that is hinted at in conscious and unconscious intentions at the outset of the poem, and what they know intuitively about how this particular work fits into their more long-range formal intentions. The thoughts that occur as they are creating a poem, like psychoanalytic interpretations of the elements of a dream, that on first sight may seem disconnected, fragmentary, and insignificant, often best illuminate poets about their intentions. Sometimes the poet will later introduce these thoughts into the poem itself.

Yet these self-disclosures may put pressure on our willingness to trust this bizarre demand for confidence. From the beginning of the poem we realize that not only may the poet disappoint us but she may also mislead us. Out of this conflict and tension, sensing the pull of her reader's anxiety and absence, the poet evokes from her being remnants of her private existence to remind us, along the way, of her particular vulnerabilities. Yet it is just this process that is likely to wrench the poem from the domain of convention and rhetoric. Such resonances may add to her poetry more authentically and spontaneously the harmonic overtones and kaleidoscopic facets that are perhaps more tactfully obtained through irony, baroque vocabulary, deliberate primitivism, camp naiveté and "dumbness," repetition, and charm. Imagination in writing poetry becomes continuous with a way of paying attention to the juxtaposition of related thoughts, a way of figuring things out — even, and perhaps particularly, her "personal" problems. For it is by weighing and exploring such considerations that she effects the choices that will or will not enhance her imagination. She discovers "by accident" the actual recurrent objects of her fantasy.

WRITING AS REVERIE

"I've got a feeling we're not in Kansas anymore."
– Dorothy to Toto, *The Wizard of Oz*

1. An obsessive monitoring of some remembered texts becomes an immediate occasion for delay, association, structure, plentitude, a gathering for an album constructed out of items of intrinsic value. Play conceived as the manipulation of reminders, an accumulation of fragments, passes through coherence into speculative fantasy. The argument runs like this: a child, pausing before his book, falls into a reverie. This daydream, composed in part of excessive thinking about power and mastery and a concurrent, if hidden and counterpointed, theme of loss, an anticipated, almost yearned-for loss, becomes equated with a particular visit to the ocean on an overcast day. The objects employed in his fantasy are transposed harmonically and modally into its emotional leitmotifs. The visual complements the emotional tense but cannot surpass it. The child is not exhaustively reading the seascape. His eidetic imagery is fastened to the concepts preceding it. Entranced as he is in his thoughts, his actions contribute to an air of unselfconscious movement. A momentary breakthrough of sunlight between clouds interrupts the melancholy quality of his meditations and the spell is half broken, because we see him again engaged in reading. Or is he merely seeing the printed words, his gaze still directed within, as the sound of the sea thunders loudly into his consciousness and the voices and activity and movement rush into his field of attention?

2. Meditations on an esthetics of fragmentation and discontinuity. Creation of a myth. History before me an interpretable reminder. The politics of extension and intentional fragment.

The interruption of "the argument runs like this" is a simple dimensional loosening of the referential register this particular moment of writing needed. Anywhere I look (for example, at the child on the beach at sunset) I pass through a storm of connectives, intensifying one another.

3. Holding the entire thought over my head like a cartoon bubble in the comics. Head scrambles neologisms. Each face inscribed like a photoengraving on the surface of the page. The age of portraits, the gradual acceding of biographical identification. The inscription, the latest removable naming of the surface crests. So the completed thought now resembles the boy's hesitations on the title he gave to his text. Notice it was found in a book of art manifestoes. He likes maxims, tautological witticisms that temporarily acquit and illuminate with guided opacity the steady pointed shadings toward the outcoming familiarity of the chosen puzzle: is he dreaming of the words themselves, divided as they are with each selected entry seal illustrated in a deluxe edition of signs?

4. "They can see right through me," thinks the child. They can diagram the

space anyway they like, but I'll know by the tempo of his excitement whether or not the molecules might later collide and issue a fusion of opposites. Say the original imagery was not a naming, but an identifiable entity suspended above his head like an exclamation point. Not the subjective reticence of the *I* signifier, but a fire (!) and consequent, simultaneous engendering of excited tension. Bound up as he is in reading, he is perhaps for the first time equating a description with a given locale in a book — he is on a certain beach not yet named. He is reading his thoughts specifically against, next to, behind and above this presentiment of a later time when he will item for item inscribe this sea in his album, by means of partial, token representations.

WRITING AND REMEMBERING

History is a catalogue of endings, but poetry speaks of being, of beginnings. Through an experience of linguistic recreation by immersion in a semantic continuous present of simultaneities, echoes, symbols, variously shaded fragments of raw and refined perceptions, the text (and its corresponding thought process) is momentarily liberated from its history (memory) and from its history-making function (remembering). This is why poetry is relatively free, compared to related disciplines like philosophy and psychology, from its own history. Its elements, including its formal properties, are subject to aesthetic, but not temporal, critiques. There is no linear historical conceptual development in poetry — only a process of eroding and building.

Poetry tends to have an ambivalent relationship toward any temporal function to which it is assigned. Unlike most other human endeavors, at certain moments, often its best ones, it cloaks itself in obscurity, withdraws from everyday life and takes the form of a static, receptive object. A process made to be acted upon, germinative, wood and oxygen waiting to be ignited by a determinant, though not necessarily parallel, flash of thought. And this is how it transcends history and is not only to be recognized and remembered, but contemplated, like the Sphinx.

Writing as remembering is nominative, ordering, and elicits from its reading a fixed, functional relationship. But poetry can be composed of any number of continuously altered, modulated and interrelated emotional tones, purposes, and intentions. These real, apparent, and illusory intentions are usually consciously parodied, at least at some point in a poem, if not in the form itself, creating still another shifting ground of contexts.

Historicity, that is, the legitimation or authentication of a work or event by establishing its historical relevance, binds language to fixed significances by ordering its syntax into descriptions of familiar or unfamiliar sequences of related perceptions or memories. Language, though bound to time by its passive connection with the process of recall, can be made to listen to itself. Again and again heard differently, through its poetry, language directs attention to its plastic and iconographic qualities by means of a kind of lexical hovering in and around, and subterranean plummeting through, meaning and memory. Familiar connotations, meanings, and connections fade into apparently new ones, ones otherwise too close and familiar to sense and feel.

To read poetry is to enjoy a mimetic gesticulation towards the thought process, to demand from it alternatives to ordinary remembering and comprehension. In this elusive, decorous, and ceremonial absence of significant reportage, history is a minor character in a timeless masque enacted in the evolving theater of language.

WRITING AND IMAGING

Because remembering is often involuntary, it constantly juxtaposes images and fragments of thought spontaneously into the thought process. For this reason, remembering continually transforms the effect of specific associations and images on the meanings or symbolic values we assign to certain thoughts as we write and reread what is written. Since remembering causes such transformations by overlaying, condensing, and displacing associations, this process prevents the permanent linkage of images to specific associations. Such mutability in the length of time images may be linked to specific associations in the thought process also makes possible, in writing, by methods such as juxtaposition, aural association, repetition, and physical placement in the text, the alteration of their character, symbolic value, or relationship to the composition as a whole (their "scale"). As the composition proceeds, written images, as mental projections, are continually re-scaled against other images by the transformation of lexical associations. The harmonic, rhythmic, and symbolic values of images undergo changes in scale depending on the lexical and aural association chosen by the reader or writer to be, at any given moment, their signal source or "key."

Of all types of writing, poetic discourse, like the psychoanalytic technique of free association, tends most to cause the experience of remembering to be idiosyncratic, personal, and dehistoricized. By the latter term, I mean that the stories or fantasies elaborated from the texts or associations may be constructed or deconstructed at any given moment by current associations. The method of free association flattens out the relative value of images by placing them in a one-to-one relationship to consecutive fragments of ideas, unlike purposive forms of thought patterns fixed by sequential ordering. Chance and random sequencing of images can have a similar resynchronizing/desynchronizing effect, by causing shifts between coded message readings of the fragments and the intermittently phased current "readings" of present images looped into signal words and thoughts. Specifically, the difficulty in poetry with imaging is that after-images often tend to be sustained in remembering much longer than is necessary for the most musical, rhythmically modulant grouping of sequential or juxtaposed signs. Too transparent a statement, meaning, or purpose might scale down, for instance, a group of signs so radically as to make their source overtones too minimal to have any impact on the composition as a whole.

When the word, object, sign, and trace synesthetically embrace the mind and the page, associating symbol with its mark, title, token, signal, and glyph, symbolic value's rigid hold on meaning is weakened. The image's source can again have a monitoring, signalizing effect on the way meanings and intensities of meaning are assigned. The modally transformable image is one that is subject to the shadowing, tinting effects of one meaning juxtaposed against another, layered on and under it, like the creation of an approximate sign in lieu of foregoing any possibility of recollection. Or one fixed sequence of meanings may be transformed into another register by creating new associations in a mutation or variation of the text, by, for example, reversing one part of the sequence and allowing one set of symbols before that part and after that part to remain the same. In writing this may be an alteration of syntax within a customary phrase that could be translated back again within the thought process simultaneously, or almost so, as the text is read, just as an inflection or modification in speech might entirely alter the character of an expression in relation to a purely syntactical form of the same idea. Again, the resulting transmutative effect would be caused by the feedback between a meaning and an intentionally added reframing of its tonal value, affecting a shift in its remembered, historicized meaning.

THE TALISMANIC VALUE OF WORDS
IN PRIVATE THOUGHT

Writing requires an effort of the mind to sustain a narrated sequence of images of objects and ideas for the purpose of communicating them in an informative and comprehensible order. Long-standing absences of mind, possible when reading (where the mind might follow word-code signals, nouns are familiarly patterned, and the details are exemplifications) are not possible when doing conventional writing. Maybe wordlessness of mind, imagelessness, led to the creation of "ennui," the reader's malaise, this sickness of communication raised to the form of a type of illness. Blankness is the real experience every writer knows best, most convincingly written about by such writers as Kafka, Pavese, and Valéry in their journals. Because of its receptive and passive character thinking often trails off into blankness. Attempts to think rigorously often lead to enumeration of instances, evidences, naming and classification of these evidences, and symbolic transformative modes like mathematics.

Nothingness is often the result of mental conflict. Robert Motherwell once wrote: "Blankness is the failure of alternatives to come to mind." In the emptiness of our minds words pass by, sometimes unattached to their original contexts, juxtaposed, chaotic. It is strange how often thoughts have so little to do with our verbal and written communications. The apparently random quality of thought may frighten us into being too cautious. Naturally we must struggle to use words to coordinate activities much the same way we use mathematics to order the machines that produce our necessities. But neither the machines nor this stupendous creation of social language have helped us very much in our overall relations with one another. Might not a big part of the problem stem from our use of language as a social instrument or "machine"?

The mechanical mode of using language — grammatical meaning — makes it possible to share information efficiently. Most of this information has to do with the manipulation of objects. But we might notice that while we are exchanging information we are simultaneously controlling the energies of certain word-associations to link up the word with its object, much as the object is invested with a totemic relation to its owner. Still, words have an existence completely their own. They are objects that can be studied archaeologically, as real as diamonds and limestone, and reveal much about the process of thought.

Reading poetry points the attention of the mind's eye to this aspect of thought: that thought's relationship with language may be compared with the relationship of objects to their space. The "space" of language is thought. Outside this space, language is in a world of objects. What takes place during such a drastic movement of the objects of thought from one habitation to another?

The substance of average thought actually has little need of the imaging association of nouns. This is clearly seen in poetry. Blake's tigers are images of an image, seals warding off the entrance of the eye back into the world of objects that exists behind the use of language as transparency. Behind those tigers is the world of the dream, the tigers of Rousseau's jungles. In states of revery, meditation, in moments of pause between actions, thought is less likely to be molded into the totemic currency of direct representation of value. This sort of language is weighed and measured symbolically. The transformation of physical relationships expressed in the form $E=MC^2$ attests to the cosmic implications of a coordinated exchange and manipulation of objects derived from a pattern of linguistic signs. The substance of thought when unattached to such weighing and measuring is often experienced as a reversion to a state of wordlessness or disconnectedness of associations. Reading regenerates the purely manipulable powers of language. Contemplative thought reverts to language expressed in an idiosyncratic, personal code of such weighings. This personal code is difficult to translate into a socially adaptable exchange system. It is far easier an alternative to impose one's own value system on the world, or to equate one's own values to some aspect of what is "out there."

The value of thought in its relation to language may lie in its possibilities for obtaining freedom from a slavish appropriation of social language for ordering and defining itself. The value of words may be brought more closely into the unmanipulable domain of personal use and away from the named, the de-finite and its ally description, the ordering of memory in the form of anecdote, history, the record, the absolute proof. That this talismanic use of language is not attached to objects in an ordinary social way is frightening because it casts one's relationship to words in an utterly personal way. Its expression in art is a totemic value of great significance because it returns words to their archaic potency in the imagination. In this way they evolve a personal hieroglyph of which one's poetry is an emblem in a universe of individual minds.

The personal value of a myth of one's own thought lies in the freedom of the mind to explore its own domain. This is how the creation of poetry secures the poet's word-totems. At the same time, one aspect of the awareness created by such a wrenching away of language from social ordering is its glimpses of the unique terrain of the individual mind. It is not simply a reflection of the images of what words represent in socially agreed upon usage. Revealed in the act of excavation in the world of thought, words are recharged in their totemic value and the mind's hieroglyphic coding system is transformed — signs on the cave enclosing the opacity of thought.

WRITING AND EXPERIENCING

Writing is unbounded by paradigms, and its paradigms are subsumable to, and consumed by, its forms. Associations to a poem's instances are not fixed by its formative instants, to the intervals of perception, thought, and experience the words designate. Another reason why, technically, the poem and its elements have no history, no *precedents*. The poem and its elements revive an obsolete definition of that word: prognostication, presage, sign. The words prophesy their return in other spheres of experience. They are repeated as a mirror reproduces a silent effigy of an object, and as one harmonic liberates and proliferates its possible modulations. The preceding transformations appear to lead inevitably to a moment, a lyrical configuration that is not only discrete but is also an interval, a transitional point in a rhythmic succession of moments.

*

They repeat themselves, not as a mirror echoes its content, but as one harmonic sound liberates a set of possible related modulations, and simultaneously lends those previous to it the quality of having engendered something unique and specific, despite the irrefutable evidence of the senses that the moment was not discrete, but part of a continuity.

*

Ravel and Debussy: The musical dissolve — sudden sonic wipeouts of the interval just heard — sudden lyrical expression or quick aside in writing, a parallactic mode of self-definition.

*

The functions and character of paradigms in poetry are both qualitatively and quantitatively different than in any other writing. Aesthetic intentions are usually paramount, whether the actual instances cited are expressed for historical, emotional, musical, visual, philosophic, political, or personal impact. In no other art are these relationships so delicately balanced and so easily misunderstood. In and of itself, for the poet, the production of any poem or any element in a poem constantly brings the question of the purpose of the paradigm cited immediately to the fore. For this reason, the pulls are strong toward the Scylla of historicity and the Charybdis of obfuscation. In the former the paradigm seems clear: like the poet, the poem moves through the sequential media of time and experience. Since there is no opposing paradigm for poetry — or experience — this is possible and technically acceptable. But the danger here is that another paradigm is, in a hidden way, even in a deceptive way, being reintroduced. That paradigm might run like this: since I am a poet, my consciousness is a poetic process and instants of that consciousness are markings on a map of my poetic geography. Technically, this is true, and even necessary to take into account when writing poetry. But when this mode is established as a paradigm there is a radical reduction in the scope of a poem and the scale of the elements are too rigidly established vis-a-vis each other.

*

The chant and the song elude the limitations of linear narration by means of the "haunting" refrain. Through harmonic repeating, reverberating, echoing, and iconographic alternation the "flicker" effect of language transcends the "flat" character of historicism. For historicism, ambiguity is a threat, as is projection, because it is experienced as intrusive, too immediately and suddenly intersubjective, and not easily subject to the ordinary processes of remembering.

*

The mutative relationship of poetry to art is akin to that of philosophy to science, science to technology, technology to the art of communication, art to language arts, etc.

*

The problematics of space = the problematic of the human relationship to space.

*

The same for matter and time.

*

What is the relationship of this problematic to the appeal of density, or rapid experiences of strong emotional impact directly juxtaposed against the material facticity of language?

*

"My sense of language is that it is matter and not ideas — i.e. printed matter." (R.S. June 2, 1972)

>*The Writings of Robert Smithson*, edited by Nancy Holt
>(New York: New York University Press, 1979), p. 104.

*

Writing is fixed and sustained in media like paper, stone, metal, and plastic. Experience is fixed through reenactment and is sustained by emotional memory. Writing and experience have dissimilar flows, partly caused by their dissimilar media — one static, nonhuman, and inorganic; the other alive and recognizable by movement. Only the experience of reading adds an experiential dimension to writing. In any case, like a forgotten ruin or monument, it continues to haunt us in its facticity as object. But the immediate presence of the sign, which changes humanly as we reflect on it, is revealed prismatically in its paradoxical relationships to memory, and thereby to actual experience. Printed poetry can emanate an aura of graphic monumentality, not so much in memory, but in reading, particularly in rereading. So that rereading adds a new dimension to reading — the shifting, parallactic quality of poetry is related to its projective devices. These give an overtone, an afterimage to the time directly before and after reading poetry, of meaning that is akin to the meanings derived for assessing experiences, but not its exact double.

*

The prevailing distinction between poetry and rhetoric illustrates one ordinary instance of the *au courant* literary distinction between "writing" and "writing about." But the difficulties some people have with the fragmented in art is similar to the preference for the long prose poem (which apparently has all the virtues of the energy implicit in a rhetorical flow of writing without rhetoric's disposability) to the short poem. So "writing" would be synthesizing its own structure while "writing about" would somehow be presupposing some external referent or axis of explanation. Poems are universes because of the parallactic relationship of words between, and words within, languages.

*

The poem and the reader are equidistant from the meaning of the poem.

*

My secret: to know that I am withholding something. Your secret: to know that I am withholding something.

*

Remembering is partly an encumbrance the art of writing carries due to its synthesizing function in the formation of memories, and history (sequencing of experiences).

*

As historicism partly collapses in the movement generated by technological advances in both recording and retrieving memory traces (like the recovery of the icons of Tut and the hieroglyphs of ancient Egypt and the encoded languages of the contemporary computer disk) language continuously revives its function in writing, through its power to reflect the full range of representations of experiential reality in the mind, and in its familiar, obscure, human experience of thought and feeling. Language today (as depicted in Godard's *Alphaville* and *Weekend*) is the enemy of the State and historicity because of its power to germinate systems antithetical to custom, since custom is partly dependent on coded laws. Historicism, while allying itself with writing, knowing its enlarged scalar power as a reread document, distrusts its projective character (translation: instability). Taking language truly seriously as a partly known, partly unknowable form of energy is instantly recognizable to historicism as an antithetical challenge. Historicism debunks efforts to reify poetic language, except occasionally in art and artist's texts on art (as in the manifestoes of Dada). Words closely seen are mirrors of consciousness, tones of thought and feelings, traces and bones of human experience and not simply mechanical reproductions and manipulations of the processes of memory, of the visualization of the causalities of historical development, the interlocking links of historical narrative, the imagistic jigsaw puzzles of traditional poetic formalism.

*

Even though most fiction and theater would have it the other way around, there is actually no point in personifying the essences of human experience. For reenacted experience to speak to us in an authentic language it must be a phenomenologically apt version of intersubjective and intrasubjective relating between people. It cannot simply mime the faces, gestures, and expressions that seemingly stimulated its conception. It is for this reason that poetry is ultimately the most realistic of all human expressions in that it places literal clarity and empathy about psychological, political, and existential viewpoints to the side of encompassing, in all its variable senses of exemplification, the pure essence of experience. Of course in purely temporal terms, this is a very long-range view of practicality. Other sorts of practicality certainly have their uses for human endeavors. Still, the signs of these gestures, the naming of moments that instantaneously codify human communication — "we all see this" — we imagine we connect to these feelings in memory. Memories are followed by language like paths leading in from various directions. Though the faces of these moments are their histories, the inner core of consciousness is not a film or mirror but a series of hieroglyphs. It is a map — a specific array of markings — lines and points and variable distances and durations: ever wandering, oboes babbling in counterpoint, in memory following the motive of the main and developed themes curiously dogging them. Wandering touches of felt experience enfolded by the inner thoughts surrounding them — not one, not even a thousand voices could fully characterize that resolution. It is heard in one voice, but it is spoken at once in all languages that is its own language.

*

Poetry reconnects the occurrence and the instance.

*

parallax — the apparent change in the position of an object resulting from the change of direction or position from which it is viewed.

*

tide day — at any point, the time between two successive high tides.

*

We can get an approximation of experience through words in that memories, because of their subjective character, reenact the meanings we apply to experiences, just as when we read we reenact the meanings we apply to a sequence of words. When we say to ourselves, when reading, "That's how I feel" or "That's how I see it myself," we are often tempted to underline the words we were reading when we experienced the feeling of comprehension. Yet then, strangely, when we reread the underlined passage, often it no longer contains the meaning we imagined it held.

*

"There is no need to be astonished at the part played by words in dream-formation. Words, since they are nodal points of numerous ideas, may be regarded as destined to ambiguity."

Sigmund Freud, *Interpretation of Dreams* (1900)

*

Experience is spoken not only in its own key but derives its language from all aspects of every element of being. Writing the experience, writing about experience, writing. Language creates itself out of the necessities for marking the trail — to mark a path — but it defines its own aspects of reflection on or from itself, its umbra. As commentary and accompaniment, companion, map and decoder, the thought process in its daily use is too often recoiled from — especially when it is dense with multilayered ideas and fantasies, or criticized as "too" intellectual, "too" inward, narcissistic; it is as if thinking itself were worse than watching television, or reading, or seeing movies, or writing about experiences. For the poet, thinking *is* writing.

*

The power of an idea does not solely consist of its groundedness in being.

*

"I further had a suspicion that this discontinuous method of functioning of the system Pcpt.-Cs. [perception-consciousness] lies at the bottom of the origin of time."   Sigmund Freud, *A Note Upon the Mystic Writing Pad* (1925)

*

Reading, like perception, fades out and in. But it would be more correct to say that it juxtaposes simultaneous types of thinking that are ordered in a way similar to the way sentences join together words of different types. As if illogicality could get you there, thought reaches out for, but is touched by anyway, the places some of the thoughts travel to that words don't reach, exactly. Waves are repetitious — thought is repetitious — something like tides. No two exactly the same yet their times are predictable. The moon stays exactly the way it is, slightly offsetting the full gravity of the Earth. Steady, but, understandably, not perfectly steady. Also, thought must be reordered into grammatical order. Yet it never quite keeps up with the latest stylistic requisites. Its beauty is not exactly the same as that of language. Thought is free but alone in its freedom. It can't be fully socialized — yet it can compare its truth to that of language.

*

"Timelessness is found in the lapsed moments of perception, in the common pause that breaks apart into a sandstorm of pauses."

Robert Smithson, "Incidents of Mirror-Travel in the Yucatan," p. 94, The Writings of Robert Smithson.

*

Writing offers to experience a third eye, a parallactic measure and scalar key to the relations between communicable and noncommunicable states of perception and being. Reading offers to experience not a mirrored double but a third voice, an harmonically variable scale that may in the literal sense graphically represent states of being, just as a certain grouping of notes may "represent" alternative modes of enharmonic and intervalic overtones. Polyphonic *ekstasis*, the reading experience translates a multiple text of felt interactions. Experience is read aloud, reading signifies a return to silence. Writing is enshrined in the heart of experience. "All life exists to end in a book." (Mallarmé) The ending is contained within the beginning at every juncture, which contradicts the impulse to equate reading about experiences with actually having them. Writing, by revising experience, transposes involuntary memories into present ones. In advance, the mind, set on record, transposes what would be free associative and dreamlike states into statements. Returned to the workings of language, experience is felt to be on the other side of the mobius strip. Reread, language is a hieroglyph of experience, but a script both of experience and silence, blankness.

*

Equals=equals==. Scratches are the equivalent of signatures, the spirit of the totem's reification is retouched, carved, and wears away. Spoken aloud, thought is heard and felt, is touching, moving.

*

> being carried along
> was supposed to be in form
> when the replica began to face
> before that, time is (was) imprecise
> exactly itself without moral tones

*

By listening awkwardly (not like in conversation where the overtones are potentially embarrassing) this voice declines concentration on the dictates of one particular stage in the argument. While the observer has an eye in unremitting concentration on the inevitable, the reader is deftly persuaded to reenact, in silent assent, the genesis of an apparently random sequence of images.

*

I can't use the predictions anyway. I see them only in retrospect.

*

Instances follow one upon the other, invoking an internal sequencing of experiences. The substantiation of these instances framed in an accumulative pattern forms an aggregate point of realization. The ideas that emerge most fully contrasted within the aggregate constellation of scaled images stimulate conceptualizations about the presumed presupposed internal structure.

*

not . . . . but

WRITING AND CONCEIVING

Natasha: They ordered me not to see you again.
Lemmy: Who? The Alpha 60 engineers?
Natasha: Yes.
Lemmy: What makes you afraid?
Natasha: I'm afraid because I know a word . . .
   without having seen it or read it.
           — from *Alphaville*, a film by Jean-Luc Godard

All experience is conditioned by expectation. The meaning of an interval of experience is defined throughout by the implied or covert meaning of its end. The tension of an interval arises out of the anxiety of evolving a meaning for an event. Debussy confounds this process in his music not by employing an obsessive doubting or repetition of themes, but by allowing a focussed uncertainty to remain. The rhythms are not halting or arbitrary, yet they may be felt as not quite intended, or as distracted but determinedly so, not just tentatively. He gains the continuity ordinarily obtained through a form that tantalized with eventual resolution by arousing different levels of dreaminess and wakefulness. We wake from a dream to enter, clearly, a daydream.

*

Writing ordinarily stresses its function of "righting" the meanings of words and word combinations. But the graphic materials of writing also have a mapping and marking function. As records are evidence, the reified word is a token of identity.

The sign distributes the imaged perception as an imprint transferable to the "scratching" of thought against the cave walls of the mind. Signs transmute imaged perception into thought: at the terminus points, always approximate, always tautological.

Each subdivision of an interval is discrete when it is noticed over time, but the remaining subdivisions are more blurred when specific ones are selected for focus. Similarly, a grapheme within a nominal phrase such as a headline or a title would be conditioned by the phrases subsequently selected for emphasis. In present consciousness any subdivision of an intervalic constellation can exist in any combination of the three temporal dimensions or is apperceptively consigned to temporal mutability. The same it true for the relativity between intervals of script and all the hierarchical organizations within the text. The more general inscription (such as a headline, a title, a chapter heading, or the capital letter at the beginning of a line in a poem) conditions the mode of focussing the related text. The equivalent in remembering is the hierarchical arrangement of significance. The base word of significance is *sign*.

Poetry is a graphic form of unrighting the publicly codified collocation of grapheme with symbolized ordinary writing and speech usage and the imaging function of the mind. The conceptual experience of a poem causes a reconnection with the acausal, atemporal conceiving of meaning by reapportioning the relative values of the scalar organizing function of the perceiving process and the inscriptive, defining level of preconscious verbal imaging.

*

It is a certain tone I am after, embellished by persistent, varying shades of association. I repeat it as I am hearing it in a kind of suspended listening, paying attention to and allowing to dissolve certain obsessive memories. Deductions, or rather, reductions or vapors like these, afterwards seem immediately familiar, precognitive, felt throughout an extended deja-vu atmosphere during an imploded time sequence. The puzzle is attempted only once in order for the observers to immediately witness its decomposition. It is a simultaneous recording, unwinding and playing, joining and dismantling, similarities momentarily continuing to hold sway throughout or just long enough after an initial and suddenly heightened series of contrasts. Such points of connection are heard in specific invariable tones and intervals. The names of these sounds and feelings may be the objects and words memories attach themselves to. But the feelings that yearned for those names, the ones that offer themselves later as keepsakes, are really more memorable. Not the images which are now absent, but the thawing and sketching around that in coming times will be added to the fondness that grows around such replacements for the quality of the actual event. Anonymous, the words and exalted rituals plaintively repeating them.

Lexic qualities of
Semantic qualities of
Signal qualities of
Structuralizing qualities of
Quality of constructibility into family systems
Genealogy of
History of connection with lexic qualities of meaning
Graphic qualities of
Quality of distribution

Distribution of naming to order spatially
Distribution of naming to remind
Distribution of naming to induce
Distribution of naming to attract
Distribution of naming to direct connection to
    identification

Naming that orders
Naming that connotes possession (control, ownership)
Possession of names
Erosion of names
Ambiguity of names
Plurality of names

Naming, identifying, recording, delimiting, describing, describes, humanness of, clarifies, evokes feeling, vocal qualities of, musical qualities of

*

The activities of the mind associated with the recording and verification of the relationship between identity and physical space are governed by memory and the verbal technology necessary to preserve it. To repeat (chant, sing) the poem is to elicit a vision of prophecy. The function of poetry is not only to enlighten but also to point us in the direction of the mind for the source of that enlightenment. Poetic composition is an activity that subtly alters the rules that govern the relationship between the ordering of thought and allowing it to swoon into reverie. Remembering is at its base a connective mode of cognition. From this is expropriated its power to order, to value, to record, to create, to historicize, to catalogue, to describe, to recreate, make safe, controllable, and distant — to signify.

*

As many times as I try to grasp my solitude, I am abruptly thrown into the image of the Other and its absence, mute spectator. Or just as suddenly to stop, trapped in the spectacle of my fear of his or her absence, the patient, responsive, loving Other situated to the side of all that is depriving. To switch so suddenly is to plunge into the mercy of a simple truth: as neutral as the irrational is the subtly perfect, the preposition of all impostors, clown of confusion, enigmatic signature of incomprehension.

*

18. Salvaged debris.
23. Moisture, remainders, dew, condensation.
24. Reference points on a map, questions of materials, accident.

*

All reading experience is summoned forth in the mind of the writer. Against this recital of thought lay all the significant moments of speech — from the first cries to, and from, the mother to the syntactical complexity of the most heartfelt account of experience — these moments mark the boundaries of one's language.

To read is to practice a mental resonance between language, thought, and memory. As in ordinary thought, to read need not simply be to systematically connect mental processes to their current context but also to other, related aspects of present or past experience. Such an idiosyncratic variation in reading any text is inevitable, especially in rereading.

Memory becomes history when some constellation of events still triggers a strong reaction while the specifics are fading as the memory recedes. History is necessary when memory threatens to fail. Memory is aroused by emotional and physical need. As culture (apparently) changes more rapidly, more attention must be concentrated on the meaning of the shifts. When we are insecure about the memory function we invoke historical (ordering) paradigms.

*

Sometimes I allow somebody else, in some way, to speak through me. I know the somebody else is me, but I also know that some information is coming through that perhaps was picked up peripherally, or has been forgotten and is silently colliding and thus combining with something else. The other voice during the conception of a thought before the wording has taken on specificity. A high altitude photograph and then a zoom-in for details. This permits initially irrelevant details to later enter the framework.

"The scale of the Spiral Jetty tends to fluctuate depending on where the viewer happens to be. Size determines an object, but scale determines art. . . . When one refuses to release scale from size, one is left with an object that appears to be certain. For me scale operates by uncertainty. To be in the scale of the Spiral Jetty is to be out of it." (p. 112, *The Writings of Robert Smithson*, New York University Press, 1979.)

*

The sentence is a prison term
Why poetry made of fragments
Irreducible crystal forms
Lesson. Intermittent continuous connection
That's why subtract (subtext) poetry
Instead of abstract
Seems made of starting
Hemisphere at images
Spring-like or spring

Remembrances
A pause, faces opposites
Little askew, a tilt
Framing reflection out of
Mirror, less a, wanting, unwound
Each vulnerable, venerable
Split atom

Cars   Skates
Bikes
Trolleys

*

Writing is reading. I live in a world of signs which acausally direct my consciousness. Thought is writing, just as thinking is protolinguistic. Thought is
reading just as listening enforces a transposition of an interval of related
sounds into a specific inner focus of attention. Writing silences a babel of voices each of which calls attention to its own point of origin. At the root of all
comprehension exists an indeterminate number of possible meanings that are
coming into being, into consciousness. All understanding or visual or aural
recognition contains within it an underlying chaotically disordered core in flux,
moving as a system of connected points toward an entropic state of inertia, a
stable pattern.

All systematized language is oppressive insofar as it supports ideologically
based repression. Repression serves psychic economy. To "forget" the origin of
a meaning, or its specific and unique context, is to suppress energy directed
towards associative expansion and purposive expression, that is, the purpose is
blurred as is the associative gestalt.

Thinking, reading, and writing are forms of preconscious play. Thinking
itself, which is imagined to accompany reading, is synchronistically tilted, one
moment toward, the next away from experience. Like speaking, reading, and
writing, thinking is imagined to be a translation of experience. But this translation does not completely evolve apposite to experience. The sign constantly displays its maddening ability to outwit its supposed "associated" thought, and as
its creator seizes on the reminiscence of its genesis, the acausal connecting
process of association determines the actual signification. This eventually
becomes the "meaning" of the experience. These meanings ordinarily are interpreted in intervalic measures of "beats" of time. Meaning entropically moves
toward "familiarization," which is static, rather than "defamiliarization," which
is nascent, and closer to the fulcrum of the acausal axis of interval (instance)
and pattern (generalization).

*

You lose the actual qualities of the experience when you try to be too precise
about the specifics of each interval of the flow. Any exhaustive rendering
becomes a compilation of instances. The historical perspective makes instances
appear less improvised than they actually are. The decisive moment, the dramat-
ic realization, is itself a heightening of the particular instance from a valued perspective. One examines what one wants to know thoroughly again and again.
This is called testing, experimentation.

We wait and try again. We measure and take note. We generalize and enu-
merate. We sift through. This sifting, this remeasurement of experiences, one

combined with another, leads to connections that are imbued with the feeling of discovery, that are re*mark*able.

Now, as I look out through the porthole of this ferry, even from this distance, I am thinking that one small rectangle of graduated color, yellow white to pink to black, to specks of, pinpoints of, electric white light to blue, brings to light, to mind, the entire dawn.

THE INDETERMINATE INTERVAL:
FROM HISTORY TO BLUR

(written with Alan Davies)

Event-related signals can reveal subtle differences in mental processes. The wave that appears when the mind confronts nonsense is easily distinguished from the one that results from simple surprise, according to Dr. Steven A. Hillyard of the University of California at San Diego, even though there is surprise in encountering a word that transforms a reasonable sentence into nonsense. He and Dr. Marta Kutas reported discovery of the coping-with-nonsense signal recently in the journal *Science*. This signal appears about 400 milliseconds (four-tenths of a second) after the event that causes it and appears on a graph as a negative voltage. It is called the N_{400} wave. The brain's signature for surprise is found in another wave called P_{300}, a positive voltage appearing 300 milliseconds after its event.

The newly discovered signal seems to appear in response to a nonsense statement, even in prolonged testing, Dr. Hillyard said. Even after encountering many sentences that degenerate into nonsense, the brain evidently cannot stop trying to make sense of them. The special response to nonsense does not appear if a word is simply misspelled, but only if it is a legitimate word used in a nonsense way.

'This N_{400} wave seems to be tapping into a higher mental process than any that we've been studying with ERP's during the past 10 years,' said Dr. Hillyard. 'It depends on a person having a sophisticated language ability.'

– The *New York Times*, March 11, 1980.

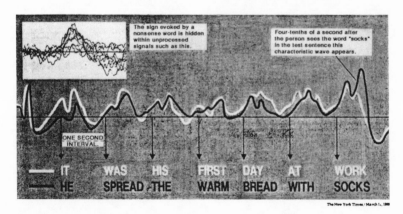

The sign evoked by a nonsense word is hidden within unprocessed signals such as this.

Four-tenths of a second after the person sees the word "socks" in the test sentence this characteristic wave appears.

ONE SECOND INTERVAL.

IT WAS HIS FIRST DAY AT WORK
HE SPREAD THE WARM BREAD WITH SOCKS

The New York Times / March 11, 1980

It was not until forty-five years later that Heisenberg stated in a new theory of physics what Mallarmé knew in 1880: "A Dice Throw Will Never Abolish Chance." Heisenberg demonstrated that you cannot measure a particle's speed and its location at the same time; out of these factors evolved a theory of indeterminacy, a theory of constant uncertainty.

> Stochastic: (Greek, *stochazein*, to shoot with a bow at a target; that is, to scatter events in a partially random manner, some of which achieve a preferred outcome.) If a sequence of events combines a random component with a selective process so that only certain outcomes of the random are allowed to endure, that sequence is said to be *stochastic*.
> Gregory Bateson, *Mind and Nature* (1979, p. 230)

The Freudian theory of free association inscribes a stochastic situation: the analyst asks the analysand to speak every thought entering his or her mind, the analyst sifts those thoughts through the analyst's mind, at some point stops the flow, selectively. Free associations, the random component; the analyst's interpreting intervention, the selective.

One interprets, with fairly great certainty, a probable outcome; the position of the individual units is relatively unknown. The relationship between writing and reading also describes a line of uncertainty. Published writing locates, within a historical moment, the position of a thought.

In metric reading (i.e., reading at a certain momentum) the reader reads the momentum; in contrast, within the Mallarméan idea, one reads the space as a schematic that resonates between two sets of intervalic waves: one, the originating creative energy that generated the poem, and two, the vibrations of the mind in the presence of the poem. In prose, the language locale is not determined; within the poem's determinations, momentum is very clear. What is actually read is scattered throughout the moment-by-moment information; the reading is continuously a prosodic furtherance of the text.

The use of associative rather than fixed descriptive language keeps open the experience that is the original and repeated referent. If momentum were substituted for place, a symbol, a representation, certain details of the experience would be left open that would be forgotten if fixed in precise and linguistic terms.

Free association — "evenly suspended attention" — is precise, working a wider field. The Mallarméan layout of words allows for a wider field of concentration. The specific words of prose are not determined by spacing. Satie's furniture music, though simple and delicate, permits the mind to take it(self) an enormous quantity of places. Each Satie note is a pointer in a possible direction, a precise and enjoyable structure of attention. Volume of attention is not insisted upon by the music, but is permitted.

Duchamp: "object" language, "language" objects. A thing associated to its idea: an equation between the object and the language about the object. Surrounding objects remind us at all times of symbolic movements within. In the presence of objects, the two are never completely divergent from each other.

1900: the seeming enigmatic (the mysterious) as a different way of getting inclusiveness, with the precision of all-inclusiveness. Over-focusing on the fixing of the historical particular, in memory, misses the field productive of the original particular and cuts off evolution of new particulars that might have come from the original field. A particular thing is the model, the example, the convincing thing within what is said. Around 1900 people began to realize the historical view to contain a distortion: leave the focusing to the reader. Both measure the specifics and grasp the sensations and experiences behind the laying-down of those particulars, to invoke the original experience, the originating state of mind. It is the difference between an exhaustive list of particulars and a schematic performing a number of exhaustive lists of particulars (which permits to anyone their filling-in). The power of persuasion, the power of giving the experience does not come from the photographic, the documentary, the "accounting."

*

Memory becomes the place, the locus, relative to which particulars get filed (both senses). Filing a thing whittles it, by putting it in that one place. Fitting in, placing things between, relates to the idea of interval. Fragmenting produces interval. The interval has a place, fits into a larger whole, a larger continuum. But it is still a very specific moment, productive of an instance of pulse, a measure, like sonar, a metronome. Intervals pulse, inscribing the certain amount of distance that has been gone through.

In Duchamp's *Network of Stoppages* (1914), the measure is inscribed as part of the structure; the structure is presented as an instance of mental measurement.

Periods (and in the grammatical sense) of history: the envisioning that *that* would exist makes it happen, the consciousness of periods makes history. Uncertainty and doubt create much more truth in the renderings and findings; "this is it," the schematics, the suggestive things, the connectives. . . . by the time it is fixed it is changed. The act of fixing is time-consuming, time-altering, time-debilitating; it shifts what time means, stops the flow (this constitutes the argument with history). A grasped history is lost when the only concern is to keep track of it in a precise way. Without the ability to measure place and momentum equally and at once, nothing really happened. Intervals are not confusing, they are allowable of confusion, in not distorting chaos.

The Egyptians personified in their pyramid building the type of consciousness that wants to totally expand the scale of human time in the universe versus the actuality of that chronology. The time becomes something in which human terms of death and life are altered dramatically by the externalization of scale.

*

Time is investigated in investigating the possibilities of the interval (Mallarmé,

Debussy, Ravel, Satie); the experimentation determines what can happen within a certain interval, without spoiling the composition of the whole: the point is made in a moment. The work assumes attentiveness without demanding it; the work values the other, trusts its reader. The work distributes not points but the process of distribution; the reader also distributes the activity.

Mallarmé's mysteries, ellipses, vectors that are not followed through or that establish themselves suddenly and curiously in a place where they had not been expected, value the activity of their reception unrestrictedly. Williams's statement "No ideas but in things" is rigid, minuscule, a limit, a sort of advertising slogan. Persons exist in the midst of ideas, even choosing to represent ideas. Interval gives an impression of scope, the absolute size of the idea, rather than an assertive focusing on the self-importance of the particular. Because thought is experienced in intervals it is possible to move from the somewhat willed and somewhat random places that are reached in thinking, volumes of distance in space and time.

Around 1900 the mapping began of the variable distances with possible volumes of thought, to note the volume implicit in those distances that constitute it. The particles are wonderfully multifarious, but they change; the distances, the relationships, obtain for new particles, new particulars.

*

The lines composed of short and longer lines are the threads.
The places where they meet are the stitches.
Language is the needle.
Thought is the thread.
The cloth is experience.
The place where the stitches meet are memory, history.

> interval: 1, a space between things: a void space intervening between any two objects; as an interval between two houses or walls. 2. a period of time between any two points or events, or between the return of like conditions; as, the interval between two wars; an interval in fever. 3. in music, the difference in pitch between two tones. 4. the extent of difference between two qualities, conditions, etc.

Art that does not push to where it has to go, that is more intervalic, admits of indeterminacy. (Morse code/computers). It is a function of attention (see *A Note Upon the Mystic Writing Pad*. Freud, 1925). The way attention was looked at, what attention had to be for things to be discovered, for attention to be attention, shifted around 1880 to 1905. For attention to be discontinuous was no longer for it to be an attention that was not rigorous; taken into account was what attention is, the way the mind works. In studying people with neurotic minds, Freud studied what was fragmented, he studied intervals. Neuroses are intervals, static on the line. Static becomes a part of the music; in that random component, for that part of the stochastic thought, enters the new thing, the other, from the other thing; from the other person, from the object, from the other person, from the other the other thing. The other music must be unidirectional, not bipolar.

At the subatomic level, almost existence, or forever existence, or other existence, is as much a part of the regular flow as is the "regular flow" itself. What almost happened, happened. There is an art that includes this blur, demanding focus: the level where the virtual, or the about-to-be, or what came before, or what almost existed but without extension, is as much a part of measurable reality, of experience. Choice breaks the flow, must be part of the music, is part of thought.

We know discrete things before knowing their names as objects. The object state is the blur between the thing and the word: beginning to perceive that a word is getting attached to a thing, the photonlike almost-being of either, is as much a apart of the world as the thing and the word and later the fact. The mind also sees the names as having discrete qualities before knowing what the word represents. The word itself is at first a thing, then becoming an object representing an object. The words are early seen as also a world of objects. The turning of meaningful sounds into words parallels the turning of thing into object. As each process progresses, words attach to objects increasingly. The process never ends; learning a thing and a name of a thing happens again in every single interval. The name of the object is not on hold. One reexperiences this less as time goes on, as experience becomes less new; one continues to notice it first as a thing, then as an object. In calling into meaning phrases or words or language that is read, the process of focussing from the original conception of what was meant into, e.g., a conception of what the author means or, e.g., what is assigned as the personal meaning, is the continuous process of the intervalic. Intervals are moments off-rhythm between the identification, interspersed into the identification, happen as often, are as much a part of it as the "it" is which is the goal. Art admits the blur towards which it was called into being. Keep it in moving, blurred-action, sense. Static: no static. Some of the focussing is seen in the creation of the text (imparting an appearance of ambiguity, but) actually holding in the ambiguity that it moved from in trying to eliminate the blur existing before the final thing was there. The blur is a bath into which the writer-reader relationship constantly dips itself; the bath consists in the movement in consciousness from thing to object-representation, from meaningful sound to word, from morpheme to phoneme. Those movements are mimed in the writing-reading process, an immersion in the development of a consciousness: the mind of the modes of writer and reader. Stein: that genius is reading and writing equally. The interactive process mimes experience more convincingly than a writer's giving of a script; rather than which the intervals extant at the moment of creation, the original blur. The work is a moebius strip, a three-dimensional figure of the infinity of this process. The slight unravelling *when* codifying, remember the original unravelling more ragged than the unravelling thing of the present, capture more of the essential original unraggedness. It would not be a moebius strip because there are no continuous lines.

> The uncertainty principle reveals that as we penetrate deeper and deeper into the subatomic realm, we reach a certain point at which one part or another of our picture of nature become blurred, and there is no way to reclarify that part without blurring another part of the picture! It is as though we are adjusting a moving picture that is slightly out of focus. As we make the final adjustments, we are astonished to discover that when the right side of the picture clears the left side of the picture becomes completely unfocused and nothing in it is recognizable. When we try to focus the left side of the picture, the right side starts to blur and soon the situation is reversed. If we try to strike a balance between these two extremes, both sides of the picture return to a recognizable condition, but in no way can we remove the original fuzziness from them.
>
> Gary Zukov, *The Dancing Wu Li Masters* (1979, p. 111)

*

Looking for the locus of something, defining its place, fixing it, also fixes an actual instance of time. The locus is a specific place that fixes; fixing on a perspective finds a moment in history and thus the unit of language in which it occurred.

Association occurs on the grid of experience: one pull is towards place, which leads towards time; the other pull on specific association is towards its meaning, the generalization that comes out of its meaning, and its structure. An association tied to a place or a mapping grows out of a pull against its meaning, generalization, and structure. Where and when a thing took place grows out of familiarization, a part of learning; generalization, the other part. The direction towards acquiring facts and knowledge and learning, through familiarization, builds up a kind of transference to that style which is what is meant by the ego. The memory function of familiarization is historicity; the other direction of the association is towards its meanings, its generalization, and the actual structural part of the mind of that association. Each pull is a relief from the other's pressure and at the same time a stress on the particular association.

An epoch in the life of a thought can be likened to an accent mark over a vowel, which is also a place mark; it indicates a certain kind of place, a certain emphasis (the lines on a topological map, grammatical oversimplification of that actual fact of height above sea level). Accenting occurs in the same kind of locus as topological marking; the plotting of everyone's enunciation of an acute mark over the vowel e at the end of a verb would produce something approximating the thing which says 150' above sea level.

Say place, names. Names place, place place, names names; place locus. Saying "here's the spot" names it, locates it, defines it; it also establishes the who of saying it, not what is said. It is a total temporal statement. "This is Kansas but, not anymore! Now it's some totally other place. We're still calling it Kansas for the sake of convenience, but it ain't Kansas no more."

*

There is a place that you are going from and a place that you are going to; to get to that place, that tracking, is as worthwhile as the endpoint of going, because while you are going there you find other things and those things are related to the final place; that helps to define what it is when you get there. New combinations and connections are experienced. In finding your locus you redefine it again each time, systematically finding new coordinates. When you try to solve the meaning of a work and you examine it looking for that spot, this tracking is what the composition is. You make a new grid to get there, but that new grid is today's grid, a new place; giving you a new coordinate versus the one you are looking for, a new name, a new meaning. It is always constantly destructible, or deconstructible. If you view the bride of language as the seductress or seductor of language then you view it as the reader and the writer at the same time. Which posits them in the same place at the same time, the text not so much a map as a median for that unity of place. Does the train for Brighton come at 2:02 or is 2:02 the time when the train for Brighton comes? The reader and the writer are in one place, as a seductor or seductress of language; finding each other, being each other being both, being one, being language. On the way to seducing the bride (or the groom) of language, differing types of separateness exist, and then a unity, then a new separateness, a new unity. (It is at that point that confusion about publishing arises, raising the questions of which road one is on relative to production.)

*

Field reading involves thinking about place in relation to meaning. Field reading relates to a reading of musical notes, to connecting the dots; to the gestalt reading; the mind takes certain evidence, accounts for it. The mind takes the dots of place factors (whether they can be put in an index, in a codifying system) which are themselves a field that the mind uses to connect them; it is already assumed in the thing that is happening that the individual moments are not historicized because one need not later know their precise position. The position is only needed immediately, for the time being, in order to get to the more general picture. Nonetheless, the dots do have a place; one could historicize around that particular place and build back up from the original impression. In field reading one has both: you can fix it, or you can unfix it later: you can fix it when reading or experiencing it but you can also disassemble the original impulses because the original fixing remains. The individual elements are given as a field in which they can be perceived separately or in which the field can be perceived as a given, as a piece of evidence, a fact. Field reading involves the factualization by the reader of the given particulars. The reader does not need to remember what was just read but can also remember it in its given position.

The originating positioning is itself approximate, but going back to a specific particular or grouping of particulars, the original relations are still maintained. It is a matter of scale. A particular grouping in a text permits the reader to retrace the meaning of the originating moment through the positioning. Giving the reader this field experience provides the possibility of the mind's, e.g., expansion of any grouping. To permit this reading the writer eliminates the historicization implied by the impression that the particular graphemic points are historical; their momentousness depends alone on the fact that their position communicates.

Dada reverses historicity: the historicity becomes the meddling whimsical random element that is consciously introduced into the flow of the interval, in a reversing of ego. Dada does not substantiate history; instead it presents an experience of specific random moments being what they are, still with specificity and still with the randomization. Duchamp reestablishes as one perception the seen field and the meaning within the mind, the multiple levels that constantly pulsate and fluctuate between the two, allowing for a multiplicity of connections; a trace of specific groupings remains within that multiplicity, the shape that happened at that particular moment in history. Dada reverses the historical within chance, the random component, the indeterminate. The modern notion that one has so much to do with what one imagines as having happened at a given moment is very much a part of Dada. Dada also saw chance as an element of history, recognized it with laughter and understood the limitations of too much historicism coming from any one direction.

That which takes into account the aspect of the ludicrous allows for a distancing from the subject material that makes it easier to experience. A writing unwilling to become ludicrous is unwilling to deal with its own specificity in time. The ludicrous permits relief from the awareness that a historical moment is the only time that permits its knowledge. If the gravity of the moment outweighs the accessibility of the knowledge, that is the pathetic.

Field reading looks for hidden connections in two otherwise irreconcilable areas, often with ludicrous results. A field reader makes the greatest possible use of any absurd connection between the particulars, making unforeseen connections out of the apparently ludicrous. There is always something to retrace.

There is an element of the mind that reshuffles the signals it experiences, reads them in different orders. Dreams and much art perform this function, a function already built into and part of the blueprint of perception. In making an art that attempts to provide for a field reading experience, one opens up to a perception of that part of the mind which screens experience. Field reading allows for the normal capacity of the mind to reshuffle experience, to see connections other than those which were thought when the mind originally formed the connections; field reading permits the mind to portray and perceive the actuality of reality as experienced.

distortion in the process of focusing is focused on minutely so that the distortions themselves are the primary focus forcing the singular point (the sign) to intersect the matrix of time/experience

The constellation that forms the original pattern of what the reader tries to retrace: any point in the text permits the other points. The splicing of two parts refocuses them in a different way; focusing a small detail that may seem a flaw or snag in the whole fabric, discovers the points of tension, the points of most resistance. The mind, in its barest function, takes in the facts, sifts them, determining both its own daily need of facts and what it must do next; it finds those things that have the most gravity. The mind grows and links to other things when the unexpected things are linked; it scans elements, processes them and in doing so, reshuffles them for another something that the mind will invent. The mind evolves a blueprint out of what is already there, does not recognize where to go next, then explores and enumerates the possibilities, a part of the mind insisting on making the ludicrous connection. The odd connection permits a reexperience of what was originally recorded but not really experienced. The mind (language) reshuffles its fragments in order to attain the original hierarchy; reassembling its permits reprocessing from the new perspective.

Language in its structure is the transitional element that is held between persons; it cannot be dismissed. In holding language commonly, persons build up a protective and necessary conventional code, as in all law, to try to equalize and stabilize and make as respectable or negotiable a currency as possible. There is understandably among human beings an enormous hesitancy to allow for aspects of language that have been held in check, to change the code of survival.

WRITING, IDENTITY, AND THE SELF

Just as Gertrude Stein conceived a distinction between "entity" and "identity" in writing, Charles Bernstein has put forth a view of writing that would free it from "self" as an organizing principle:

> Writing (or reading) that uses the self as its organizing principle, either through a persona or through the more open field of consciousness mapping, appeals to as artificial, as socially constructed, an entity as expository writing's appeal to logic.[1]

Here, and elsewhere, Charles Bernstein has also espoused a notion that an individual's freedom is delimited by a concept of writing that uses language as "a disappearing act that gives you the world on the other side."[2] Yet this view of writing, the "disappearing act" view, also implies a view of the self which does not wish to interpose the self between the reader and the world. The writer is thought of as a neutral medium, presenting his or her experience without the interference of personal "mannerisms" or idiosyncrasies. It is here that Bernstein attacks a powerful form of repression by society and helps point a way for a liberation from such constraints. Freedom from stylistic uniformity for the sake of some mythical objectivity is not to be earned under the banner of some equally mythical version of individuality or romanticized concept of "self."

It is true that the notion of the self as an evolutionary process may be illusory if the writer, the person so seeing themselves, simultaneously delimits his or her freedom to develop by adapting a co-opted view of language and action. For by this approach, the self confines its longing to break from its constraints by accepting a view of language only as a mirroring function. Charles Bernstein and other writers with a similar viewpoint understand this as a form of narcissism which actually leads people to enjoy their freedom mainly in the form of grandiose fantasies:

> "... what else is a person anyway but a signifier of responsibility for a series of actions   if a self is anything it is what that self does with its body   does with its mind   and that responsibility is for what you do not for what you go home at night and think you'd like to do if if if if one day   some time".[3]

While I agree that disposing of this form of nullifying narcissism is laudable, and that it is supported by a concept of self which is hypocritical, by defining the whole concept of self reflexively, and thereby narrowing it philosophically, Bernstein has apparently underestimated the complexity of the self-construct.

The mirroring function of the self is indeed limiting and limited. But an important theme, a complication not completely worked through in Bernstein's work, may be illustrated by a distinction that can be made between self and identity.

In Franz Kafka's *Metamorphosis*, for example, identity, and not only self, is revealed as an exquisitely vulnerable aspect of being; in Charles Bernstein's work, identity is approachable through its intimate, highly internal relationship to language. This is recognized by him as a paradoxical situation, in that language is a publicly shared entity in both the artifactual and the instrumental sense. There is no private language, in Bernstein's view, but there is an inner, fleetingly experienced linkage between language and identity:

> "A different person almost by the way you gag your reflection, or actually getting up and walking out, so predictable always the same sort of pressing with the sound of way it falls. You wear your birthday hat as a particular sequence, primarily a texture..."[4]

It is highly difficult to describe the texture of identity from the outside in, so to speak, as compared with the texture of self. Heinz Kohut writes in *The Restoration of the Self*:

> "The musician of disordered sound, the poet of decomposed language, the painter and sculptor of the fragmented visual and tactile world: they all portray the breakup of the self and, through the reassemblage and rearrangement of the fragments, try to create new structures."[5]

I contrast identity and self in this way because it is possible to understand the entire being of a person as a dynamic process of becoming when one aspect of being, which I am calling identity, may be visualized as potential and virtual, and other aspect, self, as actual and thus biographically determined (historical). In "Out of this Inside," Bernstein's style allows for a full evocation of the vulnerable, fluctuating identity in its formation and dissolution, surrounded by the refracted bits and pieces of experience in which it is reflected. Individual access to identity is attainable by means of a responsible acknowledgement of the self through its relationship and connection with others, through the expansion of alternative ways of comprehending meaning, and the recognition of one's personal access to the tools of language. This discovery of identity must be won through persistent effort:

> ". . . keep, your eyes, open, or on it, or in it, how do you know well ultimately you don't know — this is just my problem in learning to play the recorder: I have to look at the same time as I play, can't just take off, do it automatically, I (have to) "figure out" the positioning of the notes, I "couldn't" just play (a self-consciousness that "people,

sometimes, do" let you down, don't write or call, get in touch, drift
"irreparably" far. . ."[6]

In this passage the struggle of composition is equated directly with the conflicts
of the self aware of the necessity and responsibility for evolving its own identity, in relation to its signs, to objects and to others.

I am not suggesting that the struggle to develop identity replaces self as an
"organizing principle" for writing. I am proposing that the concept of self must
be understood as a dynamic, not a static, one. I am defining a contrast between
the two: identity represents all that is potential to the self in phenomenological
awareness, in part, realizable, in part not, in part being realized, in part, not. Self
represents that which is finite and observable in awareness. The self is the shed-
dable bark of the tree, facing outward to the world and relating with it, exposed
directly to it, and also protecting the identity, the xylem of the tree, vulnerable
and within. More vulnerable, more changing, the identity defies the imprint the
world and the self make upon it: "Glimpse immediately flashing formed with a
passing knowledge that becomes your whole life reflected. Still empty the
waves turning, movement to become an opacity as lap or imprint," Bernstein
writes in "THE TASTE IS WHAT COUNTS."

"THE TASTE IS WHAT COUNTS" I read as Bernstein's most direct
encounter with these difficult issues. "The change is in me," he writes, "the very
same sand of my childhood still confronts me."[7] This difficulty is brought about
by Bernstein's very static view of the self. He sees unchanging boundaries to
the self because he has not conceptualized, although I believe he has envi-
sioned, a more dynamic view of the self. He writes in "THE TASTE IS WHAT
COUNTS", "The boundaries perceivable in a form attended on both sides by a
border within which limitlessness lives, hung as press of confusion. I, in boundary, the very hum of it."[8]

When he writes, "Finding it in myself or just a blank space where some thing
should be: a ringing if not a peal. . ."[9] I sense that Bernstein is actually describing the self's tenuous approach towards identity. In recognizing in people's so-
called "damaged" aspects an understandable split that is traceable to the self's
multiple loyalties, origins, and divisive responsibilities, Bernstein discovers a
source of renewal, an integrity gained by allowing for a dynamic relationship
between parts. Though not always unified, consciousness is unifying, "solitary
in the way it insists on forming signs, hovering about an event, constituting and
reconstituting its meaning."[10]

TOWARDS AN EXPERIENTIAL SYNTAX

Freud's interest in the dynamics of repression, the core defense in hysteria, led him to some extensive speculations about memory, time, and the structural linkages between thought and language, specifically in the syntactical relationship between forgetting, linguistic transformation, and its symbolic representations in the unconscious, particularly in dreams. Reading such statements as, "I further had a suspicion that this discontinuous method of functioning of the system pcpt.-Cs (perceptual consciousness) lies at the bottom of the origin of the concept of time,"[1] one almost gets the image of Freud as a kind of time traveler, moving with the analysand by means of a receptive mental state he called "evenly suspended attention" through a maze of associations that would eventually shuttle both back to the experiential moment of the actual trauma. Like deep-sea divers, moving cautiously back to the conscious level, analysand and analyst would return these memories to the level of consciousness in the course of the analysis. From the observational platform now termed the "observing ego" the self would review the scene of the damaging experience and thereby discover the distortions that had since arisen within the structure of the neurosis in the perceptual system.

Dissatisfied with the therapeutic results of this sort of guided fantasy mode of psychoanalysis, Freud continued to develop ideas about technique. He considered the analysis of dreams to be the "royal road to the unconscious," and expanded his technique to include a method of interpreting dreams that combined free association on the part of the analysand to elements of dreams, while the analyst did the work of bringing these associations, sometimes with ultimate connections to early memories, in line with the analysand's unconscious wishes and conflicts as they related to past and present patterns of psychological adaptation. Continued exploration of both the analyst's and analysand's feelings in relation to the process of the treatment itself contributed to the development of ways to help resolve aspects of the treatment relationship that tended to seriously block movement through the core conflicts. From the work of early theoreticians like Sandor Ferenczi to more recent ones like Heinz Kohut, more and more emphasis has been placed on a careful handling of the emerging identity or self or ego construct as it is manifested in the treatment process. Similarly, although with a slightly different emphasis, object-relations theorists, like Harry Guntrip and W. R. D. Fairbairn, leaned towards helping the analysand to recognize the anxieties surrounding the emergence of the hidden, vulnerable inner self. This is also stressed in the theoretical work of the psychoanalyst D. W. Winnicott who emphasized the importance of not intruding on the inner core of the analysand's identity sense until to do so is a clearly fruitful step in the analysis. Without clear indications as to the value of such a step, this might not, in some cases, happen at all. From the point of the "reconstructive" approach, the necessity of recovering early memories may seem to encourage such impingements, although this is always an issue of concern for the empathically attuned analyst. The issue of historical reconstruction is still controversial in psychoanalysis and has recently been revived in connection with narrative theory.[2] In *Narrative Truth and Historical Truth* (1982) Donald F. Spence writes: "The artistic model, then, is one alternative to the archeological approach. We no longer search for historical accuracy but consider the interpretation in terms of its aesthetic appeal."[3] The problems with this approach include a concern for a thorough working-through of the infantile neurosis, and also a concern with the authenticity of the emerging self-construct of the analysand, vis-a-vis the mirroring by the analyst and the structuring of the identity of the analysand in the transformative process. The analyst needs to discriminate sensitvely between what is part of the "false self" (in Winnicott's terms) and what is solidly based on the analysand's positive, internalized self-representation. The importance of narrative theory for psychoanalysis is in just this area: what is really the "true" story of the analysand, and what aspects reflect the analysand's "true" goals and aims?

The metapsychology of the relation of the thought process to experience and to writing has yet to discover a bridge from the primary forms of free association and the analyst's suspended, evenly — hovering attention to their syntactical expression in speech and writing. If thought is delayed or rehearsed action, within whatever temporal frame it is conceived, writing is surely at least a connective methology between thought and experience. Ron Silliman writes in "Migratory Meaning: The Parsimony Principle in the Poem" (1982): "Shklovsky's emphasis on the dimension of time, contrasted with the spatial, reflects the importance of expectation in the creation of meaning in writing, whether such meaning unifies the text 'beyond the experience in words' or does just the opposite. The effect of a semantic shift is therefore both experiential *and* temporal, lying at the crux of the status and nature of meaning as such."[4] In writing's connection with the inorganic, its potential for monumentality, its possibilities for the establishment of transcendence of immdiate temporal limitations, we see aspects of its variability in scale.[5,6] A corresponding variability in scale may be observed in dreams and in the inner contraction and expansion of the identity sense in everyday experience.[7] In classic tragedy, for example, human emotions are seen in terms of their overall significance in the causality of events of great social significance. In much contemporary poetry, art, and psychoanalysis, such impact is to be discovered on the scale of the individual identity, or within aspects of the identity.

Scales of relativity (of size, for example, or time spans) are central to the identification and authentification of visual-perceptual experience. Percepts are ordinarily not only identified but are authenticated by means of a visual-perceptual scanning, or tracking, through some matrix of the field of experience. For example, in a photograph we identity the authenticity of a stiuation partly by relative comparison of scales as we see them in "live" experience. Another mode of identifying authenticity is the estimating and weighing, according to the ordinary experience of temporal duration, of the flow of a narrative replication of believable experience. The conventional adaptations of such methods of keying-in the reader or the observer to a subjective sense of the authenticity of the experience have been analyzed and explored by theoreticians in many fields. Erving Goffman, through his use of "frame analyses," detects aspects of interpersonal interactions that depend on almost unconscious and automatic non-verbal and verbal gestural languages to simultaneously deal with conflicting, competing, and complexly resonant aspects of communication.[8] Many of these framing methods touch on issues having to do with the place of the self and the identity in human experience. In physics, Niels Bohr's use of the concept of "conceptual frameworks,"[9] and Werner Heisenberg's "indeterminacy principle," present new ways wherein the matrix of human perception and human subjective experience must be correlated if we are to make realistic assessments of the significance of the new data that confronts us as a result of recent forms of conceptualization and instrumentation that present us with new images of reality.[10]

Almost all theoreticians in this area have emphasized, if only for their metaphorical power, the great influence of the development of modern optical instruments, which have offered much in the way of authenticating both earlier and more recent intuitive discoveries. In the book *Kunst und Naturform (Form in Art and Nature)*, a photograph of Jackson Pollock's 1947 painting "Cathedral" is compared with a microphotograph of Glia cells of the human cerebral cortex magnified 500 times.[11] The similarity is remarkable. I have compared both photographs to a photograph of the Chesapeake Bay photographed from an altitude of 570 miles from an earth-orbiting satellite. The forms and scale relationships are strikingly similar in all three. I believe this to result from the underlying simliarity of different types of scanning or "tracking" perception. In the photographic plates this is done by means of a dye on the cell (in the example of the brain cell) and by an infrared lens (in the case of the satellite photography). Pollock's painting methodology may be similarly understood as reproducing otherwise imperceptibly subtle nuances of his inner perception through the use of a fluid connection between his brush stroke and his physical responses to his perceptions of the inner field of experience. Banesh Hoffman wrote that Albert Einstein "tried to describe his method of thought, saying that the essential part was a 'rather vague' nonlogical playing with 'visual' and 'muscular' signs after which explanatory words had to be 'sought for laboriously.'"[12] Apparently, our sensing apparatus, which registers the presence of new information, is of much finer responsiveness than our ability to express it verbally in a literal way. New optical methods offer not only a means of authenticating what has been sensed by other means, but also powerful new metaphors for our comprehension of these perceptions. On the level of the identification of inner feelings and thoughts, Freud's concepts of free association and free-floating (suspended) attention offered models of inner observation which made it possible to describe and to categorize and communicate about otherwise almost ineffable feelings and perceptions.

However, at this point in the development of language and consciousness, we still experience a need for a relatively massive block of details in order to be fully convinced that an experience has been adequately described and authenticated. Imagine a communicative situation in which very small intervals of experience could be isolated as the seeds of new insights. This is the situation we move towards each time we are able to allow ourselves to trust our intuitive gasp of very minute and discontinuous intervals of experience. The mental need of transitional language to bind together very brief intervals of inner experience into a recognizable, describable unit of perception causes a continuous shift in perspective from intuited thought to communicable thought. It is possible that part of the intermittent pangs of loneliness most people feel at times, all the way to the excruciating, pathological versions of extreme isolation in schizophrenia, is brought about by our need to obsessively confirm our individual perceptual experience of reality in order to avoid anxiety.[13]

Deeply interested in and curious about the perceptual apparatus and its use in confirming reality, both Freud and Einstein (and in the arts, slightly earlier, Mallarmé, Satie, Debussy, Seurat, and Van Gogh) devised means to find a link between the inner imaginative conception of reality and the external reality that could be empirically measured and quantified and thus authenticated. Freud, in his "evenly suspended attention" and Einstein in his "thought experiments" found means to provide a mental process metaphorically equivalent to physical experimentation. In a sense, it is in this broadening of what an experiment can be that the methodologies of Freud and Einstein are similar. They employed the experimental under conditions where it had not previously been used.[14] Applied to extremely variable units of time, for example, these methods of experimentation revealed aspects of human experience that had previously been seen by many other thinkers, including artists, but had never been asserted and described in such a way that others could conduct the same thought experiment. In a sense, successive readings of certain kinds of poetry may be considered "thought experiments." In the Freudian system, the perceptual process of "evenly suspended attention" created the inner setting in which unconscious motivations, which were vaguely identifiable before, could now be more closely identified. The experiments consisted of free associating in certain ways to elements of a dream. Various strategies were employed to translate the visual dream symbols into residues of the actual experiences which gave rise to them. In Einstein's work a thought experiment consisted of ways of correlating human subjective responses to the measurement of time under quite specific, but physically impossible conditions, such as travel at the speed of light. Both approaches led to the establishment of powerful hypotheses regarding the processes that underlie perceptual actualities as we set out to describe our perceptual experience, to communicate it and measure it.

The theorists discussed above had another procedural element in common. While observing the effect of their inner subjective judgment on their later appraisal of the actuality, they observed its simultaneous entry into a changed temporal terrain. The flow of time itself became part of what they considered important to describe. They saw timelessness coinciding with the flux of time, and attempted to find ways of capturing and accounting for the interrelationships of past, present, and future. They also saw that as we focus on details of inner and outer experience with greater and geater interpretive intensity, we move into an ambiguous time zone. To understand the effect of one time zone on another, we may conduct scientific and artistic experiments to attempt to recreate some of the conditions of the passage of time. Scientists and artists, as a result, realize more and more that our whole grasp of experience is metaphorical. And now the new languages that scientists must speak in order to describe the future ("predictable events") have brought them closer to appreciating and finding uses for imaginative expressions of linguistic transformation, not only in formal symbolic logic and mathematics, but also from the findings of poetry, art, and psychoanalysis. The expansion of technological means in grasping, isolating, describing, and furthering the development of classifying and tracking actualities demands new configurations of language, and new systems for depicting human perceptions.

The subjective experience of linearity in time, as confirmed by contemporary physics, is a register of experience which corresponds only to macrocosmic conceptions of experiential duration. To isolate types of temporal experience with more accuracy it is necessary to take alternative projections from the side of altered successions. The model of succession in science and art is based in part, unconsciously, on the genealogical model of tracing experiences back in history to a prime source — the Father, originating God, or procreator. The usual presupposition is that concepts develop and grow over time, like people, animals, and trees.[15] This anthropomorphic assumption has, as part of its basis, the idea that good ideas succeed over bad ones in a linear developmental progression. That new good ideas succeed over bad old ones is in principle no different in its bias than the concept that bad new ideas can never replace the good old ones. The transformation of knowledge and the conceptual frameworks that "contain" and transmit knowledge is not, in actuality, a simple linear transformation. Rather we see that the conceptual framework mainly falls away once it is no longer useful, but will remain in use partially, for aesthetic reasons, much like those forms of architecture which build from the previous structure.[16]

The quality of distortion in an obsessive demand for "accuracy," "organization," and "verification" may be represented by the phenomenon of feedback in an electronically produced acoustic system. As a metronome, a beat, these underlying preoccupations provide the relief of repetition — the buzz and drone of the everyday — while the right hand, the perceptual apparatus, plays the melody of continuous experience. When anxiety is present in large quantities the beat level is heard louder and the melody stays close at hand, tightly corresponding to the beat. Partly because the mind has no "off" mode, it functions like a continuous musical composition played alongside a continuous perceptual mode, at one moment with images of external reality, at the next imaginative fantasy, revery, daydream, or actual dreams during sleep. These two modes are interwoven harmonically, disjunctively, or dissonantly according to individual experience. During many experiences it takes an effort of willful reflection to separate these modes and refine them for the use of deductive or inductive reasoning. The point at which the mind creates an adaptive fusion between unconscious or pre-conscious fantasy and conscious intention is the nexus point of a metronomic, phenomenological apperception of the "given" synchrony.

On the level of inner thought, the micro-level ("micro-" because of the specificity of individual associations), are the singular fragments of discrete experiences that interpenetrate with other experiences, via the associative matrix to evolve patterns that have significance and meaning. These are discontinuous in time, and are evoked or provoked by the associative process. On the macro- or visual-perceptual level are organized patterns, presented and represented by chronologically ordered symbolic configurations. This distinction is complex, partly because of the interchangeability of the perceptual-visual image and the actual object for the purposes of authentification and identification in the signifying matrix. It is this aspect of authentifiction and identity which is emphasized by Duchamp's readymades. Although authenticated meaning (and actuality) consists of data that can be associated with this visual-perceptual mode of experience, the micro- or intervalic level, having the function of permitting an ongoing conscious experience of our subjective participation in the authentification of the actuality of an experience, also connects us continuously with the atemporal aspect of each discrete experience. Since this aspect functions in waves, or beats, it participates in the inner experience of measuring time by providing a metronomic constant. On the visual-perceptual level, time is experienced as a sequence of instances that follow one upon the other, invoking an internal sequencing of experiences. The substantiation of these instances, framed in an accumulative pattern, forms an aggregate point of realization. On the visual-perceptual level, or "narrative" level, experiences accumulate, eventually providing a point of contrast or tension for reflection, stimulating aesthetic judgment as to the "meaning" of the realization. This meaning also reflects back on the actual structure of narrative itself, on the presumptions which created the possibility of the structure used to accumulate the particular series of instances.

A model for the practical accumulation of observational data that takes into account a mode of observation that includes a multiple tracking of micro- and macro-valic experience may be found in Freud's conception of the use of "evenly suspended attention." Freud's "Recommendations for Physicians on the

Psychoanalytic Method of Treatment" contains the following suggestions regarding technique: "The technique, however, is a very simple one. It disclaims the use of any special aids, even of note-taking, as we shall see, and simply consists in making no effort to concentrate the attention on anything in particular, and in maintaining in regard to all that one hears the same measure of calm, quiet attentiveness — of 'evenly hovering attention,' as I once before described it. . . . For as soon as attention is deliberately concentrated in a certain degree, one begins to select from the material before one; one point will be fixed in the mind with particular clearness and some other consequently disregarded, and in the selection there is the danger of never finding anything but what is already known, and if one follows one's inclinations anything which is to be perceived will most certainly be falsified. It must not be forgotten that the meaning of the things one hears is, at all events for the most part, only recognizable later on. . . ."[17] This, and a few other brief passages, contain all Freud ever wrote on the subject of "evenly hovering attention." By demanding this mental attitude from both analyst and analysand, Freud here distinguishes the psychoanalytic situation from what one would ordinarily expect of a scientist in an investigative situation. This technique recommended by Freud also has its basis in the view regarding creative thinking expressed by Schiller and quoted by Freud in *The Interpretation of Dreams*: "If we may trust that great poet and philosopher Friedrich Schiller, however, poetic creation must demand an exactly similar attitude. . . . 'It seems a bad thing and detrimental to the creative work of the mind if Reason makes too close an examination of the ideas as they come pouring in — at the very gateway, as it were. Looked at in isolation, a thought may seem very trivial or very fantastic; but it may be made important by another thought that comes after it, and, in conjunction with other thoughts that may seem equally absurd, it may turn out to form a most effective link.'"[18]

Freud's "evenly hovering attention" and Einstein's "thought experiments" provided models of scientific experimentation that replaced "linear" authority and succession with nonlinear resonance and relationship; events connect because they resonate with potential connective meaning rather than because they are seen as causally related through visual-perceptual typologies, classifications, and lists of instances. These methods of experimentation are not offered simply as methods of expanding and deepening the apperception of current experience as it is associated and correlated with connected experience-memories. "Evenly suspended attention," for example, is also utilized in the service of developing a more finely attuned discriminatory apparatus that supercedes, via the aesthetic impulse, those descriptions of a universal reality that would repress the human inner yearning towards self-transcendence, as exemplified by artistic creation. This is made clear in the two quotes from Freud cited above. The aesthetic discriminatory process, the great complement to the ethical and deductive capacities of the mind, one of the underpinnings of perceptual evolution, in our time has necessarily undergone a great degree of transformation. This is partly the result of massive changes in technology, on the one hand, and the great economic and political upheavals of our century, on the other. One result of these staggering transformations in human experience has been their extremely disruptive effect on the internal human experience of identity. It has become the task of contemporary writing, art, and psychoanalysis to provide linkages between the internal experience of the self and identity and the drastic effects of the outward picture of the actuality of human functioning provided by science and technology. In struggling to present a firm grasp of actuality, the narrative structure employed such methods as allegory, fable, myth, legend, and symbolism, all dependent on a definition of identity and self which ultimately traced its genealogy back to various religious myths of creation. Science gradually dissolves these hierarchies by means of the democratizing truths of biology (mortality), psychoanalysis (the universal oedipus complex), and physics (relativity of time and space, the uncertainty principle in the measurement of micro-intervals). Through all of these sciences, and analogous changes in methods of exploration and expression in the arts, the scale has shifted from the macro- to the micro-level of experience. It is the problem of documenting such intuitive experiences of duration that Einstein addressed himself to, by searching for more complex ways to measure and comprehend time than had existed before. With the "uncertainty principle" of Heisenberg came the idea that it is impossible to completely measure duration at extreme micro-levels because of the effect of the instruments required to do so. But in this context it is important to remember that Freud's method consisted only in shaping the mode of attention to the details, not the scientific instrumentation needed to photograph or record these details.

In searching for a model that would transcend a linear, successive one, Freud postulated the repetition compulsion (an analogy to his discovery might be Gertrude Stein's method of composition that replaced linear succession with repetition). It appeared to him that the mind offers an outlet for the frustrations of experiences and developments that do not follow the succession model as is demanded by the dominant mode of social reality. Where we do not adapt, we repeat: the process of development, then, is not strictly linear, but repetitive and cyclic as well as linear, and is often multidimensional, fragmentary, tentative, experimental, employing disjunctive choices as opposed to "logical alternatives." Where we do not complete, we repeat. However, if we cannot track our individual developments along a preconstituted line of development, how are we to evolve a common boundary of experience in which to verify and confirm our individual experiences? One answer may be to develop individual scales of perception, rough and ready sensings that are nevertheless internally faithful to the perceptual matrix, a new mode of authentification. Van Gogh's decision to use exaggerated colors while presenting a kind of visual-perceptual realism in depicting landscape and society represents a major step in the development of a new mode of psychological realism, giving a direction for evolving new perceptual matrices. The same may be said of such art movements as Impressionism, Expressionism, Abstract Expressionism, Surrealism and Dada: a literal faithfulness to the actuality of perception itself, not only from the viewpoint of the historical moment, but from that of the inner world constituted by the many agencies of the mind. It is the sphere of the authentification of experience and its relationship to the meaning of human identity that has come, in the twentieth century, to be brought into question and reexamined. In his use of things with personal meanings, like tickets, bills, and other found objects, Schwitters' collages, from this standpoint, pay heed to the ultimate investment of human value in the actual duration of time in the sphere of individual identity — to the "private" facts of personal experience. Gertrude Stein's theoretical contributions such as the "continuous present" and the distinction between "entity and identity," also stand as highly significant contributions to the development of new forms of perceptual authentification in the artistic process. The development of the need to experience the inner identity as an externally responded-to entity continues throughout life and is as basic to psychological survival as the need to communicate inner experiences in a manner that can be responded to by others. As Jacques Lacan put it: "Just as the senseless oppression of the superego lies at the root of the motivated imperatives of conscience, the passionate desire peculiar to man to impress his image in reality is the obscure basis of the rational mediations of the will."[19]

There is, of course, a history to the development of what we now experience as the human identity. Its function in human organization, now basic to a myriad of human institutions and services (including science, law, technology, economics, politics, the arts, psychology, medicine and the media), has its origin in the need to coordinate and manage the tremendous number of experiences available to a being who is able to fashion tools that expand, and metaphorically represent, extensions of various aspects of human perceptual experience. In turn, this extension of the function of the micro- and macro-perceptual systems enhances the aesthetic reception and differentiation of pleasurable and unpleasurable experiences as these effect the identity sense, among other aspects of inner experience. So, along with the step-by-step development of what is termed the "ego" in psychology, the human identity weaves a pattern of its own in the texture of experience. And from the shaping of tools to the scratching of words, this being made a leap by which the very thread of the cloth would be in the hands of, and guided by, a language that would function as a multifaceted representation of the thread itself, human experience.

A relatively recent shift in perspective in this dimension of human experience took place during the turn of the last century, from the late 1800's to the early 1900's.[20] This included the development of subjectivism and self-reflection in the arts and in psychology, the interplay between internal experience, human perception, and technological measurement, and human awareness of and interaction with areas of reality that had only been intuited before, including the ultimate physical constituents of matter, its inner structure, and evolution. Such insights helped transform, by an act of psychological self-reflection, the view of humankind as the puppet of fate in a cosmic drama, into a microcosmic version of a child's view of the overwhelming emotional influence of parenting, on his or her inner life. This and many other shifts in scale, brought about by the acquisition of knowledge about ourselves and the universe from a myriad of perspectives, has greatly shifted the meaning and place of the identity sense in everyday life for all people. Job's identity was fought out on the cosmic level in the conflict between the ultimate powers of the universe. Another shift came, in this century, in the uses of thought and language in relation to the meaning and place of identity within the human organization of social systems, and in the syntactical language of experience, time, and perception. With this transformation, a syntax both of written langauge and speech develops, one that more and more closely follows the weaving shuttle of human experience, from the timeless, microvalic level of fantasy, intuition, and prophesy to the visual-perceptual ordering of time and physical reality. In this shuttling, the fragmentary experience of the disjunctive association promotes the inherent dialectic of the many aspects of individual identity, making it possible for the identity to experience cohesion and still retain the needed sensitivity to change that evolves new configurations.[21]

LANGUAGE AS ACTUALITY

To assume the existence of a mental structure (an unconscious) is to elevate inner language (thought) to the status of an actuality. As thought is witness to experience, language is testimony to the real. Testimony and actuality; language's double role likens it to other resonating, interacting systems of relationships between roles, child/parent, teacher/student, citizen/state. These interactive systems grant visible outlines to otherwise intrinsic characteristics. In the overall exchange between the poles, or polarized roles, in the holding back and giving and taking, a passage is created between inner and outer. Seismographer of experience, language tracks and follows this passage, at the same time creating its own subterranean geography.

As the bearer of experience, language is active. It tells and orders, organizes and frames. As a repository of experience, language is passive: it goes underground, recedes into the background, available for recall, but otherwise invisible. In this shuttling from active to passive, from conception to inception, from experience to memory, there is a fissure, a beat, a gap, an interval allowing space and time for doubt or certainty, projection, transference. With this same movement comes the interrogative, the quest, the question: you feel it, think it, know it is real, but is it actual? This eternal questioning is at the root of all obsessions, for which, in Wittgenstein's view, philosophy itself exists, as a kind of therapy to remove "mental cramps."

To elevate language to the status of an actuality in all its forms, inner and outer, is to remove doubt by fiat: to grant it full value as evidence and testimony. The mind is mined. The inner life is granted a value equivalent to physical reality. Perception is restored to a central role in the apprehension and acquisition of new values (as it did under the aegis of its status as window to the now obsolete "soul").

To grant an intrinsic actuality to the thought process is to revive the rapidly dying function of language as an arbiter of authenticity. To offer the status of actuality to all inner experience is to remove the necessity for dependence on the idols of mediation. Where only seeing is believing, obsessiveness enters, creating in its wake countless demands for certitude — precision, accuracy, records, proof, history. As if any document could contain anything other than the values of he or she or those who created it, let thought explode the fragments of words into as many meanings as they can contain, prohibiting any one form of understanding or definition from gaining hold of their meanings, and in this way the distribution of their powers. But truth has no name, no matter which words are given to express it.

CURRENTS OF ATTENTION
IN THE POETIC PROCESS

"The Object Is Poetics"
— Francis Ponge (remark attributed to Braque)*

I glance around the room, directing my eyes in various, apparently random, ways towards this or that object. At the same time I am trying to concentrate my attention and focus it in order to grasp, to *apprehend* my thoughts. The dictionary defines "apprehend":

> 1. to take or seize; to take hold of: in this literal sense, applied chiefly to the arrest of persons by legal process, or with a view to trial;

> 2. to take hold of mentally; to perceive with the mind; to understand;

> 3. to fear; to anticipate with anxiety and dread;

> 4. to note; to learn by observation; to discover by experience.1

The definition reveals both the importance of this word in describing conscious experience and, less obviously, a way of seeing that our verbal description of many uses of conscious attention to the thought process is combined with images of anxiety, dread and extreme forms of human control.

As I concentrate, trying to apprehend my thoughts, I try to take note of them, to discover them by experience, to take hold of them, I may also fear them and try to *arrest* them. There is a cue in this to alert ourselves to aspects of attention's vulnerability. This vulnerability is revealed in the experience of attending to and apprehending thoughts in the face of every conceivable distraction. The inner complexity of the dynamics of the process of forming an attentional focus is nowhere more evident than in any systematic attempt to direct it towards an objective to which there is an internal or external resistance.

As I glance around the room, my eyes darting from this to that object, I follow my thoughts, struggling to locate the place, to arrest my attention, to stop it. I'm reviewing my thoughts, paging through them hurriedly, attempting to pause at the locus of greatest significance, meaning or resonance. At just this juncture, my attention is often divided into two or more currents, as the thought process now is tracking points of connection in as many various categories of actuality as possible, or at least as is necessary, to apprehend the sought for reality. All literary forms are, from one perspective, bounded, representational "circuits" for some process of utilizing the attentional focus or beam.

* See Notes

With the discovery of free association and the psychoanalyst's corresponding "evenly hovering attention," Freud created an axis between mental attention and speech that utilized many functions which before had been confined to drama. Some of the functions of the novel were also expropriated. Speech and writing, by means of movement of focal attention, were utilized for the purpose of mental transformation. In psychoanalysis the aesthetic motive for self-expression is subsumed by the purpose of self-transformation, aligning aesthetics with philosophy by means of a transcendent human value and goal in self-knowledge.[2] Thought is here combined with speech in a way which corresponds to writing (and all other symbolic structures) whereby the valued outcome of self-knowledge is in turn at least in part again transcended by an aesthetic function in regaining an access to the mobility of the attentional focus.

The parameters of human relating are in some ways conditioned by the parameters of human attention. These limitations are ideally, and theoretically, transcended by the apparent boundlessness of consciousness. The apprehension (in many senses of the word) of the unconscious created a new concept whereby the limits of consciousness may be redefined. Freud was able to conceptualize from many perspectives a way of reasoning that was both scientific and poetic. This was achieved, in part, by explicating and describing the numerous forms of attentional focus which can be used to apprehend actualities. Here actualities are apprehended by negating denial in all its forms, by connecting denial to repression, and by rendering unto all experiential actualities their due weight in shaping all of reality by means of their conscious apprehension through tracking their manifestations in many spheres of actuality.

Repression and denial, for example, two central psychological "defenses," function by means of diverting attention. Thus, while the mind compensates by allowing a greater concentration on other details of experience, the realm of experience which the repression and denial are covering will not "allow" attention to focus on it. This is almost entirely unconscious. The defenses include, as part of their function, a compensation which consists of substituting actions for comprehension. Thus attention is further diverted by the transformed outcome, although relief is temporarily offered by substitutions and displacements. This compensation for repression is explored in such artistic methods as surrealism, including such bizarre literalisms as Breton's image of the firing of a gun into a crowd as a surrealistic act.[3]

The expansion of inner attention to realities which have culturally enfolded certain actualities may be illustrated by the story "The Emperor's New Clothes." Since the poet is as vulnerable to the spell of accepted reality as anyone else, she or he must somehow find a way to concentrate the attentional beam on areas of experience that were hitherto "clothed" and therefore not apprehensible. In despairing of finding any help other than artistic example in strengthening the attentional focus in the mobility of consciousness, the poet must still find some way of directing the gaze of consciousness onto literally inconceivably complex and entangled linkages between various modes of experience. Then, having linked them, must hold them "long enough" or tenaciously enough to relate them with signs which resonate with them or transmit images and/or meanings which resonate with them. This affinity must be found despite the almost infinitely variable sequential orderings, transformations and variations which disguise in language by means of deceptive, illusory images, the underlying actualities.

Throughout all history with every advance in poetic apprehension of uncharted actualities, often including advances in applications of techniques and methods, came a parallel physical technology that sought to apply these poetics to everyday life. With the combined leverage of the new poetics and the new sciences and technologies, new orders of experience were reached. The frightening difficulty emerged, however that the technologies that were developed had drastic side effects which were unpredictable. It may be argued, of course, that the technologies and sciences are an entirely separate development from the modification of consciousness for purposes of apprehending poetic actualities. This is also certainly true from some perspectives, but what I wish to show is that while technologies and sciences emerge, in general, out of our comprehension of natural phenomena, and poetics emerges out of our understanding of inner experience, in general, there is an oscillation, or combinatorial of the two processes which is central to sensory and cognitive evolution. The fascination with combustion, for example, which is also enhanced by the human quest for power can be partly explained by its great power with relation to very brief durations. Human change, human transformation, as evidenced by evolutionary processes, is unbelievably slow by comparison. This is also amply illustrated by the experience of psychoanalysts, who must acknowledge the durations of time required to obtain therapeutic results through psychoanalysis. New methods have somewhat mitigated this by means of rapid, dynamic focussing.[4] These methods also operate by utilizing a rapid directing of the attention of both the analyst and the analysand on highly specific areas of focus, thus refining further the uses of free association and evenly suspended attention. Scientific, artistic and popular curiosity about methods of concentrating energy over very brief durations of time which can produce lasting effects continues, the most recent technological example being the computer. Condensation of energy by means of attentional focus has nowhere been more keenly investigated than by poetic means. This tracking of the actualities of experience constantly brings with it new forms of significant expression by enacting an alchemical overlay and blending of temporal and sensory experiences and therefore correlated forms of focussing attentional consciousness on actualities. This transformation is in turn expressed in language by new syntactic and morphological forms.

The experience of form and the forms of experience. The branches of activity that may proceed from this oscillation range from the metaphorical application of forms of technology for means of human expression (such as musical instruments and technologies for the purpose of recording and transmitting voice and music) all the way to the application of forms of movement to the transportation of human beings, animals and objects by air. Thoughts "go" through space and objects "move" through space in a cosmically graceful way, just as words may be chosen and arranged according to the aesthetic forms implicit in various actualities. The technological risk is also analogous to the poetic risk in that if an idea "falls flat" one predicted range of actualities did not turn out to actually be there. The existence of realms of actuality is, of course, not self-evident. Thus technology is needed in order to put a startling new actuality "on hold." Without the technology, we experience a combination of uncertainty and curiosity which can reach levels of extreme discomfort. Technologies are also needed for the preservation and understanding of bodily functions, as well as the transformation and coordination of a vast range of natural and human physical and communicative phenomena. The very oscillation physical/mental is ample metaphor to illustrate the interdependence of actualities for their experiential value. While great latitude is given to common sense in determining the most productive oscillations of these two basic categories of actuality, when the attentional focus struggles with the application of our technological extensions of them, we often tend to freeze into postures of singleminded applications of sensory/cognitive representational forms.

The conservation of human purposes and needs with relation to technological developments of great significance for the arts may be illustrated by photography. This technological development displaced a former function of painting and simultaneously freed painting to develop a way of focussing on the "inner landscape." At the same time photography and cinema have, for the most part, confined themselves to "realistic" subjects, despite the far reaching implications of Dada, surrealism and abstract expressionism. It is as if the child has deferred to the parent, allowing it to complete its development in dignity. Or is it that painting, seeing the implications in human terms of the new optical developments, transformed these insights into their essential representational actualities in new geometric and poetic forms? Such speculations, if they do nothing else, clarify the connections between actualities and show us that it is the combinatorial, the play of levels of attention and forms of apprehension, that gives us the clearest sense of these connections.

There is no realm of actuality upon which the focus of human attention and its denotation by signs cannot shed light. Actuality includes all that can be experienced and imagined. Actuality is the totality of all experience actual and projectable (theoretical). One of the functions of art is to propose methods of confirming otherwise elusive actualities. One role of science and technology is to apprehend, to track and to denote relationships between actualities. Einstein and Freud were both deeply curious about the way sensory experience can be expressed by thought. Each invented a special formal matrix for this tracking of resonances, Freud in using free association and evenly-hovering attention to uncover unconscious thoughts, Einstein in combining pre-verbal visual imaging and a visual/verbal/gestural resonance in his thought experiments. The primary cognitive instrument in both experimental methods was the use of an attentional focus composed of conceptual/visual imaging. Yet the lack of response on the part of Freud and Einstein to contemporaneous developments in the arts and literature outside their respective fields contributed to the idealization of action over theoretical conceptualization which has characterized the development of even their own fields since the reception of their monumental contributions.

While Heisenberg has put forth a conceptual framework which points a way out of the dilemma of the current impasse between technology and theoretical conceptualizations in philosophy, science and art,[5] his basing his theory on the positive side of doubt, uncertainty, is not exactly an innovation, if one examines it in the light of theories and philosophies of the past. Doubt is the center of human conflict inasmuch as its sublimated forms provide the intense energy needed to actualize the strange mixture of curiosity and perseverance needed for creative artistic and scientific work. To say that nature is indeterminate appears true intuitively because human beings have always placed a high priority on the implications for the future that lie in the combination of creative and destructive forces in any dynamic system whether observed in nature or constructed by people. Yet doubt has never before been understood and described so clearly as it has by psychoanalysis, particularly in comparison to those ages when it was the task of theology alone to provide a focus for the investigation of those realms of actuality about which we are perpetually in doubt.

Certainly an assertion that science, even psychoanalytic science, has no application to the arts is false. The creation of translational media to transfer the knowledge of one discipline to its useful application in another often raises serious epistemological difficulties. While both Freud and Einstein contributed new terminologies and notational systems which opened up new access routes to artistic and aesthetic, as well as physical and physiological, processes, neither could fully grasp the implications for the way they were shaping new uses of the attentional focus. It is important to recall that the arts must play both a critical and acknowledging role with relation to the sciences, while the sciences and technologies direct the arts towards complex realities which heretofore had been intuitively recognized actualities, tracking and authenticating the significance of actualities for natural phenomena and human experience and their part in structuring the current view of reality.

The implications of both Einstein's and Freud's understanding of the use of the mobile attentional thought process extend beyond the borders of their own fields. Their theoretical constructions regarding fundamental human experiences led them to examine in perhaps the most visually apprehendable, or visually/verbally comprehensible manner the relationships among thought, language and visual/verbal perception. Einstein wrote in 1945:

(A) The words or the language, as they are written or spoken, do not seem to play any role in my mechanism of thought. The psychical entities which seem to serve as elements in thought are certain signs and more or less clear images which can be "voluntarily" reproduced and combined.

There is, of course, a certain connection between those elements and relevant logical concepts. It is also clear that the desire to arrive finally at logically connected concepts is the emotional basis of this rather vague play with the above-mentioned elements. But taken from a psychological viewpoint, this combinatory play seems to be the essential feature in productive thought—before there is any connection with logical construction in words or other kinds of signs which can be communicated to others.

(B) The above-mentioned elements are, in my case, of visual and muscular type. Conventional words or other signs have to be sought for laboriously only in secondary state, when the mentioned associative play is sufficiently established and can be reproduced at will.

(C) According to what has been said, the play with the mentioned elements is aimed to be analogous to certain logical connections one is searching for.

(D) Visual and motor. In a stage when words intervene at all, they are, in my case, purely auditive, but they interfere only in a secondary stage, as already mentioned.

(E) It seems to me what you call full consciousness is a limit case which can never be fully accomplished. This seems to me connected with the fact called the narrowness of consciousness (Enge des Bewusstseins).[6]

Similarly, Freud sought for connections between elemental sensory experiences by means of new ways of examining the nature of the translation of thoughts into words and pictures in dreams. In *The Interpretation of Dreams* he wrote:

Thus dreams make use of the present tense in the same manner and by the same right as day-dreams. The present tense is the one in which wishes are represented as fulfilled ... But dreams differ from day-dreams in their second characteristic: namely, in the fact of their ideational content being transformed from thoughts into sensory images.[7]

In this way, Freud shifted our comprehension of the morphological implications of the process of transformation of language into sensory images in the thought process. By connecting this insight to the use of the attentional focus in deciphering languages at various stages in this morphological process he found a doorway to the possibility of changing the nature, the "script" of human experience itself. In "Psychoanalytic Reflections On Einstein's Centenary," Erik Erikson quotes Einstein: "I sold myself body and soul to Science—the flight from the I and WE to the IT."[8] Erikson also writes about Freud's "Id" in this context. But is not this "IT" of Einstein and "Id" of Freud the "otherness" of experience itself? It appears that both Einstein and Freud intuitively understood the relationship between time and the actualities of human experience by learning to direct the focus of attention within the thought process not on words in a literal way but on the correspondences and resonances among words, signs and actualities in the pre-verbal imaging function of the mind. There is an elemental combinatorial in the morphological and syntactical structuring of language. Words, in their structure, are like Japanese or Chinese characters, or like hieroglyphs, as Barthes and Derrida have often pointed out.[9,10] Words have characters and histories which are recoverable in the same way we apprehend visual perception on an unconscious level. Einstein writes in Appendix V, *The General Theory of Relativity:*

We have seen that we feel ourselves impelled to ascribe a temporal arrangement to our experiences, somewhat as follows. If β is later than α and γ later than β, then γ is also later than α ("sequence of experiences"). Now what is the position in this respect with the "events" which we have associated with the experiences? At first sight it seems obvious to assume that a temporal arrangement of events exists which agrees with the temporal arrangement of the experiences. In general, and unconsciously this was done, until sceptical doubts made themselves felt.[1] [This footnote in Einstein's text is to the passage that follows:] For example, the order of experiences in time obtained by acoustical means can differ from the temporal order gained visually, so that one cannot simply identify the time sequence of events with the time sequence of experiences.[11]

Here, Einstein intuitively establishes a basic connection between our experience of actualities and the sensory anomalies created by their interconnected use in their apprehension and measurement of experienced duration. Similarly Freud saw recorded in the unconscious as expressed by dreams the highly complex and deceptive relationships between images derived from various sensory forms of inputting. We divine this combinatorial by focussing the attentional beam on the "station" (so to speak) *before* the literally verbal/visual one we use for speech. In this locus of attentional focus, Einstein and Freud "felt" "saw" and "heard" the nature of time as it is present in actuality, not as it is apprehended in our commonly held metaphorically visual version of this experience. They devised new modes of tracking temporal experience that could also be authenticated through visual/verbal resonances, and then located the site of this apprehension in a place where words and actualities have a different relationship to each other than the one where our attention is riveted to the moment to moment confirmation of our shared seeing of the world. In this resonance words, things, temporal sequence whirl about within the perceptual matrix, spinning out signs which combine meaning and sensory experience in a way which can be re-connected to the human experiences which formed the original attentional tracking of actualities.

The associative combinatorial consists of an oscillation between the acoustic (verbal) image, the visual (representational) image, gestural (muscular) imagery, olfactory as well as gustatory imagery. The associative combinatorial, suspended in the oscillation among these sensory elements, necessitates a synchronous fusion of elements of actuality in creating language. What is created is not only a trace of language, but a highly complex tracking system which can literally "play back" past experience by transforming actualized linguistic elements by means of the mobile, transformative capabilities of the attentional focus. Freud is pointing to the "ideal points, regions in which no tangible component of the apparatus is situated,"[12] in tracking the locus of this sensorial, conceptual matrix. The attentional beam utilizing the associative combinatorial is discontinuous because of the necessity of this oscillation. Continuity would exclude the past and the future since each sense-perceptual experience is discrete and simultaneously "touches" on earlier ones as well as synchronistically connecting to future ones. To sense where we are moving unconsciously, to utilize what is presently being experienced for that purpose, means to split the attentional focus into past, present and future. To relate seeing and hearing with the evidence of the other senses as well as the cognitive capacity and the memory function requires a system of imaging which coordinates all the sensory images available, imaginable and assimilable. As explorers of incompletely charted regions we track and strive to comprehend the coordinated evidence of all of our senses, including the symbol-making, language-making process. This concurrence of symbolic, syntactical and morphological configurations of sensed actualities points us in the direction of the actualities we wish to focus on and apprehend.

Like poetry, mathematical and formulaic equations modify the meaning of sensory elements by utilizing systems of subtexts. These subtexts define the alterable magnitude of the images associated with the signs. Subtexts are a logical extension of symbolic texts because what is ordinarily represented through repetition or duration is signified by altered scales of magnitude. In "'The Antithetical Sense of Primal Words'" Freud observes that "Dreams even take the liberty . . . of representing any element whatever by the opposite wish, so that it is first impossible to ascertain, in regard to any element capable of an opposite, whether it is to be taken negatively or positively in the dream-thoughts."[13] This aspect of dreaming, like poetic creation or mathematical creation, utilizes the actual representations as transformable elements. This transformability is activated by the transformable attentional focus which "interprets" or oscillates the elements to create an overlay of meaning and experiential representation. The transformability of magnitude, and scale, represents dynamically the actualities which lie beyond a particular reality offered by focussing the attentional beam on a composite, recogritory point of synchrony. Poetic configurations are, in part, the outcome of an attempt to reconstitute the early responses of the mind to experiences because these primary associations themselves were formed at the point in an interval of experience when the impact of the actuality had the strongest effect on the form of the conception itself. This is the moment in the morphological process when the signs themselves are closest to experience, though this gulf is, as Einstein suggests, apparently unbridgeable, by definition. It is as if at this pole of thought the mind is closest to the transmissions of external actualities, or that the attentional beam of the mind can "touch" the actuality itself. Optical and acoustic instrumentation give us means of comparing these relationships at different scales of magnitude, just as written signs may represent scales of relationship among actualities, including sensory experiences. In reflecting on the powerful effect modern recording techniques had on his consciousness, Rainer Maria Rilke wrote:

> At one period, when I began to interest myself in Arabic poems, which seem to owe their existence to the simultaneous and equal contributions from all five senses, it struck me for the first time, that the modern European poet makes use of these contributions singly and in very varying degree, only one of them — sight overladen with the seen world — seeming to dominate him constantly; how slight, by contrast, is the contribution he receives from inattentive hearing, not to speak of the indifference of the other senses, which are active only on the periphery of consciousness and with many interruptions within the limited spheres of their practical activity. And yet the perfect poem can only materialize on condition that the world, acted on by all five levers simultaneously, is seen, under a definite aspect, on the supernatural plane, which is, in fact the plane of the poem.[14]

In this essay Rilke goes on to theorize that, using the analogy of recording sound by scratching a surface while speaking into a cone, "what variety of lines then, occurring anywhere, could one not put under the needle and try out? Is there any contour that one could not, in a sense, complete in this way and then experience it, as it makes itself felt, thus transformed, in another field of sense?"[15] Here Rilke compares the synaesthetic, transforming function of poetry to a similar action by a technological instrument of sensory reproduction. He saw a hopeful aspect in mechanical acoustic experimentation in that ". . . if we are looking for a way by which to establish the connexion so urgently needed between the different provinces now so strangely separated from one another, what could be more promising than the experiment suggested earlier in this record?"[16] Rilke's suggested experiment consisted in trying to replay the "primal sounds" of humanity by "playing" the grooves he observed on the coronal suture! As a poet, Rilke understood that actualities may be reproduced by means of resonances between other proximate actualities and that such recording methods, like writing poetry, track actualities by means of sensory responses to these relationships. Similarly, Einstein and Freud tracked the nexus points where actualities are transposed into communicable realities. Memories, represented by sense experiences, track protolinguistic visual/verbal/gestural/olfactory/acoustic/gustatory/tactile images which direct us to the boundary points of the relationships among actualities. Although these actualities, like the realities which come to represent them, may not be invariant, the principles governing their relationship may be consistent and therefore predictable. These relationships are reconstructed in the thought process over and over again with each apprehension of a thought. This apprehension brings about a focus on an interval of causal experience. This focus is ordinarily what is taken to be the meaning of an experience.[17]

Although indeterminacy is one way to describe the oscillation (or discontinuity) that underlies the perceptual process, this blur is actually one state in the focussing of the attentional beam. Moving from one perceptual matrix to another creates resonances and interplay — the combinatorial interplay that Einstein and Freud identified. This attentional focus may also be directed according to the metaphors available through the optical and acoustic action of current technology. The photograph, the microscope, the telescope not only provide the means of picturing for us the external actualities but also show us how to explore, by analogy to the attentional thinking process itself, ways to track glimpses and contours of uncharted actualities. While the physicist directs attention to the speed of light, the poet is soon wondering about the speed of dark. This is the nature of the combinatorial interplay in the poetic process. As Freud makes clear in *The Interpretation of Dreams*, one function of the unconscious is to be the locus of the combining of sense perceptual data.

Since consciousness must be influenced by the mobile, attentional focus, a portion of the mind must have the function of blending bits and pieces of perceived actualities synaesthetically into meaningful configurations (a syntax).[18] All of this must be carried out by the poet in the darkness of almost conceivable and inconceivable actualities.

The act of reading itself restores the visual/acoustic pictographic combinatorial process which is the mind's "mystic writing pad." When the thought process centers on an acoustic perceptual matrix, for example, the hearing process, hearing fades out from one locus of attention to another. Signal decay may be observed in the oscillation of the attentional beam from one mode of sensory experience to another. We go from one mode of attentional focus to another by means of the oscillations of the transmitted emanations in the overlap of this combinatorial. All apprehensions of this combinatorial are analogous to the sense of touch, in some sense. These oscillations may form an exchange of energy so great as to cause a shift in magnitudes of attentional focus, condensing and fusing the sensorial apprehensions at many access points of actualities in relatively short intervals of experiential duration. It is the analogy to touch, to direct experience of the most fundamental nature, that magnifies the attentional focus in the apprehension of an actuality that had heretofore been only sensed, or intuited. Erik Erikson quotes Einstein:

> A wonder of such nature I experienced as a child of 4 or 5 years, when my father showed me a compass. That this needle behaved in such a determined way did not all fit into the nature of events, which could find a place in the unconscious world of concepts (effect connected with direct 'touch'). I can still remember — or at least I believe I can remember — that this experience made a deep and lasting impression upon me. Something deeply hidden had to be behind things.[19]

The oscillation of sensorial experience to comprehension to analogy to a technological instrument back to the primal sense experience in the apprehension of uncharted actualities is made clear in this nostalgic reflection of Einstein's.

Touch is the sense that is our most primordial mode of authenticating actualities. Thoughts cannot be touched or seen or heard. Only through some form of language can this authentication take place, by means of a correlated focus of the attentional beam. At the juncture where sight authenticates touch, touch moves from the level of direct apprehension by sensorial means to a level where its action may be recognized by another sense or combination of other senses. This oscillation of senses in turn molds the thought process and attentional process itself adding layer after layer of complexity with each permutation of the interacting senses and cognitive denotation. The medium of consciousness that responds to and in part coordinates this ensemble of sense-data is the attentional beam itself, which Freud labelled "cathexis." Freud's concept, which has not been particularly conducive to theoretical developments in the area of experience which Freud called pcpt.-cs (perceptual consciousness), is rooted in the conceptions of the transmission of physical energy of his time. This theoretical difficulty is partly related to an analogous one in physics to the wave and particle theories of the transmission of light. In any case, an analogy to the sense of touch is needed in order for the mind to apprehend and authenticate completely any characterization of the attentional process of consciousness as a beam, ray or focus. Freud's image of the light beam's reflections in a telescope draws attention to the fact that the action of the attentional focus is analogous to the action of light beams in a mechanical manipulation of those beams. In his *Freud and the Scene of Writing*, Derrida quotes Freud with regard to the locality of the sensory combinatorial:

> What is presented in these words is the idea of a *physical locality*. I shall entirely disregard the idea that the mental apparatus with which we are here concerned is also known to us in the form of an anatomical preparation, and I shall carefully avoid the temptation to determine psychical locality in any anatomical fashion. I shall remain upon psychological ground, and I propose simply to follow the suggestion that we should picture the instrument which carries mental functions as resembling a compound microscope, or a photographic apparatus, or something of the kind. On that basis, psychical locality will correspond to a place inside the apparatus at which one of the preliminary stages of an image comes into being. In the microscope and the telescope, as we know, these occur in part at ideal points, regions in which no tangible component of the apparatus is situated.[20]

Such analogies can help us to track the movements of the thought process, its circuits, its ways of responding to "reflection," as analogous to the ways some physical substances respond to light beams, to magnification, to concentration, collision and the proximity of other types of transmissions or emanations of other actualities. In the example of the compass, Einstein's finger could "touch" the action of a hidden force in nature — not depend on the eye to verify it or the ears to make sense of the verbal explanation of this action. Touch needs little or no explanation, leaving less room for doubt.

Of all the arts, it is poetry which most aspires to render experience into a directly apprehensible medium of the greatest inclusiveness. I do not mean here necessarily printed or recited poetry but the poetic state of consciousness which makes possible an expansion of the absorbability of experiential data by the attentional mind. Intense wakefulness is stimulated by an oscillation of types of mental attention — reverie, obsessive attention to detail, and symbolic transpositions (such as reversals of sequence and significance). Intensive verification of any actuality whether real or imagined, necessitates an oscillation, a combining of sense-data, which makes abstract thought necessary for its coordination and translation into various realms of experience. From this combinatorial, abstract thought proceeds, from the weighing and comparing of likenesses to an intermingling of senses in symbolic or metaphorical terms, to a synthesizing formulaic condensation into abstract notation. Experiential "replay" of the notation then yields both images of the corresponding sense experience plus the possibility of new combinatorials on an abstracted level. This yields the enactment of prediction (in science) and prophecy (in art).

Our actual experience consists in great part of what we pay attention to. This is why I would term a tendency in the arts towards synaesthetic processes and an emphasis on inner experience as a means of actualizing artistic expression as "actualist." Surrealism placed its emphasis on sectors of experience above reality or outside of reality because of its goal of exposing the illusions and delusions implicit in our shared conception of reality. But an inner emphasis has also to do with depicting inner *actualities* as an access route to the real body of the "emperor" and the empire of actual experience. Such a conception of poetics would be a call for actuality over reality, actuality consisting not only of the area of experience now available to the attentional focus, but all actualities which can be felt, and sensed in the total experiential process. World events are thus reported re-enactments of outcomes of thought processes which have commanded psychic attention. All other events are also actualities but ones for which sense experience offers direct apprehension although the thought process has no focal point, and are thus still blurred. As the poet Charles Bernstein wrote:

> The signs of language, of a piece of writing, are not artificial constructions, mere structures, 'mere naming.' They do not sit, deanimated, as symbols in a code, dummies for things of nature they refer to, but are, of themselves, of ourselves, whatever is such. 'Substance.' 'Actuality.' 'Presence.' The very plane through which we front the world, by which the world is.[21]

The poetic process actualizes experience by creating ensembles of notation which when oscillated by visual, acoustic or cognitive attention of certain types reproduce actualities of experience that can rarely be recorded or reproduced by other means. This notational system literally oscillates the attentional focus through the matrix of experience by means of a kaleidoscopic refraction of types and sub-types of representations of meanings overlayed and condensed with types, intensities and magnitudes of sensory experience. "Free play" of conceptual combinatorials is needed to provide the construction of overall principles of perception that effect findings in all fields. A more complete apprehension of broad-based actualities demands a broad-based matrix of attentional forms.[22]

SUBJECT TO CHANGE

Imagine reading as a kind of dilation of attention, allowing the mind to register information coming from more than one source. This maximizes the combinatory potential of the various sources. In this kind of reading, the goal of organizing and developing subject matter (which is to sequence meanings in an expectable way) is subordinated to the necessity of maintaining this dilation of the reading attention. The pulse of information is distributed in such a way that the mode of perceiving the subject matter being focussed on currently is itself hypostatized by the act of reading.

The physical facticity of language, in interaction with space and *its* apparently identity-less quality, in its finite representation as substance, can be oscillated by the attentional reading focus with musical and mathematical precision. This oscillation of meanings and perceptions, like a form of physical measurement, marks and calibrates areas of intersection between language and experience. An apprehension of some potential understanding of relationships can be approximately marked in this way, indications for an inner site of meanings, an interval to be further defined by further connection with other fractions of meanings. For example, a literally proximate meaning can be examined for its relationship to a nearby field of meanings. In her essay "Procedure," Tina Darraugh writes that Francis Ponge introduced her to procedural writing. She is interested in the "coincidence and juxtaposition of the words on the page in their natural formation (alphabetical order). In reference to each other they have a story all their own."[1]

Realizing and comprehending various literary values for thought, experience and language puts the writer in the position of deciding not only specific meanings for specific parts of texts but also what use the text will be adapted to in providing a setting for the reader to experience perceptions. It could be said, in this context, that the more various the ways the text may be read, the more complex and subtle the meanings can be, because it may be projected by the writer that eventually the many patterns within the blur may come to be perceived, given time and attention by the reader. Memory overlays the accumulated experiences of perceiving these various meanings over time into a "holding" pattern by weaving many partial meanings into a gradually "visible" or "visualizable" coherence.

Just a continuity of existence in the same nameless space through time elicits around any object of attention or experiential locale a kind of penumbra, a reflexive identity, as visual and linguistic associations come to rest around this apparently non-identifiably different, but specific area. In this way sections of actuality are marked, if not yet comprehended, so that a passage is made between a yet unknowable actuality and reality as we ordinarily experience it and explain it to ourselves. The poem "Man Carrying Thing" by Wallace

Stevens, which I think could be aptly subtitled "Poet Carrying Subject Matter" provides a clear evocation of the place of actuality, comprehended and not, in the universe of the poem:

> The poem must resist the intelligence
> Almost successfully. Illustration:
>
> A brune figure in winter evening resists
> Identity. The thing he carries resists
>
> The most necessitous sense. Accept them, then,
> As secondary (parts not quite perceived
>
> Of the obvious whole, uncertain particles
> Of the certain solid, the primary free from doubt,
>
> Things floating like the first hundred flakes of snow
> Out of a storm we must endure all night,
>
> Out of a storm of secondary things),
> A horror of thoughts that suddenly are real.
>
> We must endure our thoughts all night, until
> The bright obvious stands motionless in cold.[2]

Poetic creation is the result of a complex form of attention to inner experience so far as to include an outright resistance to the rational, "intelligent" organization of sense-data. Although the poem consists of perceptions and thoughts, it emerges as an accumulated "bright obvious," a thing-like shape of realizations in the form of a poem, in the cold sunrise of poetic apprehension. Whatever subject matter there may be to poetry according to Stevens it would of necessity be a theory of poetic creation itself. He writes:

> This endlessly elaborating poem
> Displays the theory of poetry,
> As the life of poetry. A more severe,
>
> More harassing master would extemporize
> Subtler, more urgent proof that the theory
> Of poetry is the theory of life,[3]

Stevens' view of subject matter in poetry sees its function as a question of philosophical focus, as a poetic way of understanding any kind of being, a foundational substructure of any ontology.

*

Two ways of focussing in search of *materia poetica*:
 1) On the accumulated facts
 2) On what keeps coming to mind

The line between experiencing reality obsessively and experiencing it freshly, anew, is a similar proportioning as between the compelling (weighty) fact and the compelling (weighty) thought. Subject matter is an account, earning interest; but it is possible to let writing breathe, let it interact continuously with thoughts and experiences as it emerges, rather than just put it in handy, consumable, identifiable, perhaps intriguingly attractive boxes (categories).

To follow the tracks of subject matter is to follow the fragments of evidence of actualities now collapsed into a scrap-heap of partly comprehensible feelings and thoughts and half-forgotten sounds and images. These are included in the subjects and objects of poetry. As Mallarmé put it in *Afternoon of a Faun:*

> Did I love a dream?
> My doubt, amassing ancient darkness, tracks many a
> Narrow branch, and these, living
> Like this in a real forest prove, alas,
> What makes us come is the ideal absence of roses[4]

*

In the development of a new theory of physical reality Einstein underscores the anomolous character of the interplay of the senses within the perceptual system. He uses the illustration of our perception of thunder and lightning occurring separately, which is based on our sensory evidence. With knowledge we come to understand that objectively this is not the sequence of events. Only knowledge can change our perceptions of reality into a perception of the underlying actualities. Both art and science do this, in part, by bending and shaping our ways of perceiving the actual sensory types of input which create what we experience as reality.

I wonder what it would mean to suggest a conception of experience that would not be durational in our comprehension of it, or in our description of it? We usually describe experiences as *moments* or a series of clustered moments as an *event*. We are familiar with such conceptions in visual terms, particularly in the static, yet potentially dynamic images of painting and photography. Poetry, in combining visual imagery with auditory imagery, enables us to create a form of experience which in turn may be used as a kind of experiential lens, itself fixed, yet capable of registering ongoing experience with sensitivity and accuracy. Seen this way the poem, rather than "reflecting" experience, offers us an experience of how to redirect our attention to experience. Once we are familiar with this mechanism, like becoming familiar with a camera, we may use our poem-lenses to help us inwardly visualize experiences, trace them, so that we may better comprehend them, enjoy them, and communicate them. In an age when the inexpressible is a commonplace, when so many times so many people have been so awed and so horrified, such approximations of experience provide, by means of accumulation and combination of part-images, the blurry outline of a sensed, but previously incompletely apprehended actuality. The limits of language in this way may be pushed past the boundary of a ready existing cultural images.

*

Subject matter-centered text: significance tends to be rapidly absorbed by the outside world; non-subject-centered text: tends to absorb significance from everywhere (super-saturated). Subject matter as text gives writing little to build on because it exhausts its significance in the value of its use — rendering the world fuller and literature emptier like a strip-mine.

It is in the nature of subject matter-centered texts to eventually be exhausted of meanings. Writing which is not structured along subject matter lines does not "face" exhaustion in the same way. Beginnings and endings of texts, as a result, depend on the reader's approach to them rather than on the nature of the subject matter. To read non-subject-centered texts is to forego the exclusivity of interest for a focus which is at once near and far, egotistic and selfless, physical and psychic, specific and free-floating, logical and transrational. No need any longer to discuss the limits of the rational: the 20th Century has provided evidence enough of this, as well as the limits of the irrational. The boundaries I have outlined here are those of an ordinarily durational and sensory concept of experience which fastened experience irrevocably to a static concept of subject matter. This concept of rational experience is anchored to reality by means of the same communicative channels between sensory experience and concept formation that are basic to the psychological structuration of all ordinarily sequential forms of temporal experience such as remembering and anticipating.

To be able to transform subject matter into words as a writer and then transform it back into experience as a reader is the alchemy of the writer blended with the alchemy of the reader. The possible permutations are immense. This is similar to the transformability of an equation (such as $E=MC^2$), a highly simplified sign, into tremendous physical energy; the writer-reader relationship, like the scientist-technician relationship, can create immensely powerful new actualities. Francis Ponge writes, in his poem "Reading the Sun On Radio":

Since such is the power of language,
Shall we then mint the sun as princes do money?
To stamp on the top of this page?
Shall we make it climb as it climbs to the zenith;
YES
So that the answer may be, in the middle of the page,
The acclamation of the world to is exclamation![5]

In *The Noble Rider and the Sound of Words* Wallace Stevens writes that "The poet refuses to allow his task to be set for him. He denies that he has a task and considers that the organization of *materia poetica* is a contradiction in terms."[6] Stevens further counsels a move away from the "pressures of reality" for the poet, who must be free to pursue this noble rider towards sound. From a political standpoint this may appear to be irresponsible. And yet Stevens seemed most concerned with the preservation of aesthetic experience and grants a poet a privileged role with relation to experience and work. In any case, poet or not, the privileged usually have access to a greater piece of the "action" in the game of language — with more knowledge of the plot, the story, the narrative unfolding, the true influences. This is a privilege, literally, of place represented by the fact that we, the audience, sit in rows gradually receding away from the action, as in the amphitheaters of ancient Greece. Ultimately, though all the circles surround the inmost core of subject matter the outer rings are less and less a cohesive part of the whole; hierarchical ordering is part of the nature of organization. The immediate cohesiveness brought about by an elimination of apparently irrelevant message receivers fragments the actuality of the neighboring universe from the perspective of the universe of the subject matter under scrutiny. This fragmentation, now part of reality, must be reflected in any symbolic rendering of that new configuration. Subject matter=authenticity=public confirmation=scientific verification. Somehow, with subject matter we often have the feeling of being left out or just barely included in the action, that somewhere else there might be, for example, more up to date material, a more authentic source of confirmation, or an authenticated furtherance of the tracked configuration. It helps, however, to remember that in all cases, no matter how purportedly neutral, it is the final word of the individual(s) organizing the material field encasing the so-called subject matter that determines its system of inclusion and exclusion. It is just this exclusionary aspect of hierarchically organized subject matter that makes the discontinuity of poetry so necessary and so appealing. Poetic experience is one of the few experiences that enlarge the range of types of attention and perception rather than sharpening its focussing power by limiting it structurally or thematically or by content. The poetic process is one of the few ways of increasing the experiential scope of language in an increasingly publicly codifed network of universally communicated and accessible viewpoints and phenomena. "What changes the day into night?" the computer-dictator asks the investigator-agent Lemme Caution in Jean-Luc Godard's *Alphaville*. Lemme's answer destroys the computer's control of language and therefore of the society, and his answer is "Poetry."

*

Where subject matter is the organizing principle of writing, organization is equated with classification, which in turn is equated with keen attention to the similarities and differences between things. This way of focussing attention and perception exercises a powerful exclusionary factor. Strong borders guarantee an effective exclusionary action — an action which encourages focus and retards combination. Organization by subject matter effectively regulates accumulation and condensation of related materials and encircles an area of experience. This is why subject matter is so related to place and is so easily adapted to a concept of place. As K.C. Cole, a writer on contemporary physics, puts it, "Part of the problem comes from our propensity to place boundaries between things where boundaries may not naturally exist."[7]

I want to move towards a metaphysics of language which shifts the creation of significance away from an emphasis on metaphorically physical conceptions of subject matter and the powerful psychological and social determinants behind the institutional ownership of meaning creation towards a conception of the actuality of language in the creation of meaning as experience. Once I ask myself to track my experience in the creation of language and not the confines of conventionally defined subject matter I feel like I am experiencing writing taking place, not the taking of words *to* a place, to place them there and keep them in their place — now everywhere.

In this everywhere which is each place and not one place, the significance of place itself no longer towers and intimidates — it's just there and its scale is human-sized and its time is yet infinite and universal. With these two foundational planes in flux, the specificity of subject too begins to oscillate, in its significance, collapses in on itself, and having shed this one focus, a kind of attention to actuality emerges during this transformative motion which, in turn, is able to focus perception differently, so that it is capable of evolving a transformable scale of times, places and meanings.

To redistribute the focus of the reader's attention in the writing of texts may help one to see that rationality itself demands that we "read" (comprehend) experience in a highly complicated way. When we read texts, there occurs an inevitable comparison, both conscious and unconscious, to the flow of everyday thinking, feeling, observing, intuiting, deducing. Texts may be constructed which follow this rhythm, for example by imitating the structure of the syllogism: major premise, minor premise, conclusion. This pattern conveniently corresponds to the organization of subject matter according to a recognizable flow of sensory perceptions, such as those obtained by visual, auditory and tactile experience.

On the other hand, texts may be constructed which resist such an expectable development, much the same way that experience at times is unpredictable. Dreams provide a very good model for such constructions, continuously offering us a reminder that conscious and unconscious processes contain a highly complex overlapping of raw perceptions and mental responses to such perceptions. Frequently, dreams draw attention either to an apparently trivial object of a perception, or to an apparently unconnected field of experience which surrounds the central focus of ordinary attention. In the non-subject-centered text, such enlarged details, intuitively brought into focus by the text's construction, increase the reader's awareness of the mobility of the attentional process, often at the price of defying everyday "logic." It is important to note in this context, that discovery and invention are also often encountered in the course of setting aside or even sacrificing everyday common sense.

Such awareness of the mobility of the attentional focus can help writers to reveal and readers to apprehend elusive or hidden actualities by foregrounding through combination and contrast otherwise unrelated perceptions. In the construction of texts, this may be accomplished in part by causing the reader to also "read" (or *track*) the reading and writing process itself, while simultaneously attending to the revelation of subject matter. As a result, the "stimulus" of the text includes not only the thematic material corresponding to experiences of "the world" outside the text, but also some thematic or formal representation of the world's impact on the genesis of the text's construction as well as it constructive principle. The writer's expectation that the reader's attention will be mobile and self-referential, as well as rationally prepared to compare the movement of the text with the ordinary flow of perceptions of reality, makes it possible for the writer to move the reading attention away from an exclusive emphasis on attending to subject matter towards the riskier process of observing inner speculations and subjective associations to the text.

*

For the most part, language functions according to the rules of physical reality as its most apparent surface imposes itself into physical reality as our means of using it as a communicative medium. However, as the experiential properties of the sign-making process emerge we must acknowledge the limitations of the subject-centered view and use of language because, in its nature, the language-making activity tends to cause a transposition, in the mind, away from its roots in substance of which subject matter is one metaphorical application. As this use turns in on itself, enfolding its own structure more and more in its turns, another structure is built up which supersedes the groundedness of language in physical substance and again turns to a wider, and more inclusive, focus. Since a basic aspect of actuality is the innerness of experience, in this way the innerness of language perpetually reconstructs itself, rising, like a Phoenix, annexing itself to sources of originating energy unknowable directly to the senses, but only traceable by some imaginative extension of them.

Perhaps the reason for the preoccupation with subject matter in writing relates to our preoccupation with the identity of things, due to our need to communicate their qualities to each other, human beings being among the most interdependent of all species. Our ability to distinguish things from each other is connected to our extraordinary capacity to survive under the most difficult conditions and to seek out ideal conditions. It seems that in the development which follows the full blossoming of this capacity, to distinguish between things, comes a refinement in our ability to distinguish experiences from one another. It is not just that the subject matter has changed. It's that we now can place knowledge about conceivable experiences more at the center of our attention, than knowledge only about things. And even this knowledge we find it most difficult to express in terms of known actualities but tend to remain with each other's external behavior as if this behavior made each other into subjects and therefore more like things. But the flow of experience cannot be understood simply by describing it or characterizing it, because this again reduces it to movements and more abstracted actions — like emotions or thoughts — which when simply described in language still fail to satisfy our need to give expression to the full range of experience.

Webster's Dictionary defines subject, the noun, as 1) one who or that which is under the power, control, influence, observation or action of some other person or thing; especially a person who owes allegiance to a ruler and 2) that which is treated or handled in discussion, study, writing, painting, etc. This synonymous connection between subject (in the sense of a person hierarchically beneath someone else) and a subject as a point or thing reinforces the notion that the subject matter way of organizing language use can be a way of denying actualities rather than acknowledging them and defining them. Of course, this way of "controlling" associations potentially focuses the attentional image-beam sharply enough to see the implications of one perspective through a labyrinthine series of developments.

In her book *Sympathetic Vibrations*, K.C. Cole points out that the two physicists Robert Wilson and Arno Penzias tracked the presence throughout space of radiation still in existence from the time of the creation of the universe. This followed their noticing a continual buzz on their radio telescopes that they originally thought was noise. As Cole puts it: "One person's noise is another person's information."[8] One way to shift the centrality of subject matter is to replace the sender/receiver model of writing with a receiver/sender/receiver/sender model where both "terminals" acknowledge their part in comprehending and redistributing information about the sought-for actuality. Conventional narrative writing emphasizes past experiences just as conventional speaking emphasizes previous experiences, as Erving Goffman has so persuasively argued in such books as *Frame Analysis.*[9]

*

K.C. Cole also quotes Lincoln Barrett from his book *The Universe and Dr. Einstein:* "In trying to distinguish appearance from reality and lay bare the fundamental structure of the universe, science has had to transcend 'the rabble of the senses.' But its highest edifices, Einstein has pointed out, have been 'purchased at the price of emptiness of content.'" In Ron Silliman's book *Paradise*, he writes: "This was and now you are constituted in the process of being words, your thought actualizing through the imposition of this syntax. Resistance alone is real (coming distractions)."[10] I wonder if Silliman is here comparing the poetic process to one aspect of contemporary psychoanalytic theory in which the central focus of the psychoanalyst is to identify the nature of the resistances on the part of the analysand to certain types of subject matter that reveal repressed wishes. This method of extending awareness becomes a way of tracking repressed subjects rather than a way of perpetuating already existing subjects. Charles Bernstein's poem "As If The Trees By Their Very Roots Had Hold Of Us" has a line in it which could aptly be applied to the sense of subject matter I have outlined here:

> "Maybe if we go upaways we can get a better
> View." But, of course, in that sense, views don't
> Improve.[11]

In order for writing to enter into the experiential territory in which kinds of perceptions are no longer literally describable but must be approximated, writing must enter into theoretical and hypothetical modes which do not literally characterize realities as they are currently visualized. The experience of comprehending experience often has the effect of interconnecting subjects so completely as to render the divisions we ordinarily think of as subjects themselves of limited applicability to actual experience.

Jackson Mac Low, in an article titled "Language Centered" writes: "Thus it may be most correct to call such verbal works *perceiver-centered* rather than 'language-centered' (and certainly rather than 'nonreferential'). Whatever degree of guidance by the authors, all or the larger part of the work of giving or finding meaning devolves upon the perceivers."[12]

Tracking a network of small, yet identifiable, markers leads to the more frequent appearance of sign-posts pointing to an ever more apprehensible new perception of the whole network, rendering the previous sub-divisions of continuously diminishing applicability. The reading of non-subject-centered texts, requiring as it does, mobile, multiple forms of attention, elicits a type of reading analogous to the way a radar or sonar device tracks a moving object. The attention is directed to a representation of the object which may be continuously transforming its movements and its apparent surfaces so as to elude perceptions unassisted by the device. The construction of the non-subject-centered text may be partly motivated by the wish to provide experiences for the reader in using, hearing and understanding words in a similar way. One important facet of this kind of language for tracking is the use of language for evoking kinds of attention, forms of awareness, rather than describing particular identities of objects or beings. Subject-centered texts tend to use an historical, a "which came first" or even "me first" or "us first" type of verbal organization as compared to non-subject-centered writing which tends to juxtapose many types of subject matter for the purpose of demonstrating that this experience or that type of symbolic expression has some relationship, often serendipitously, to this other representative expression or area of language events. Often the purpose of a non-subject-centered piece of writing appears to be to create the possibility of finding relationships between otherwise disparate meanings or experiences, which in turn can reveal suppressed or repressed actualities. The experiential text, ever intuitive, seizes on the particular. The conventional narrative, ever characteristic of visible reality, seizes on the type.

*

Subject matter organization tends to circle around discrete moments or discrete events or discrete facts. These need a hierarchy in order to relate each bit of information. *This* hierarchy may be actually more experience-distant than perceiver-centered texts. The subject matter text tends to reveal a chronology which finds continuous connections between moments, facts or events. The non-subject-centered text tends to manifest the discontinuities inherent in experience, tracking instead, connections made apparent by the awareness which emerges out of such transformations of states of being. "The purpose is not to disclose the real essence of phenomena but only to track down, as far as possible, relations between the manifold aspects of experience,"[13] said one modern physicist. And Walter Benjamin: "Continuity in historical terms is that of the oppressors. History for the oppressed is one discontinuity."[14] And Bruce Andrews, from his poem, *Jeopardy:*

> Words were what were whole what wasted
>   words want
> waiting whose travel there- tips threats necessary
> noise nothing needed noise noise not order[15]

And Tristan Tzara:

> We are often told that we are incoherent, but people intend this word to convey an insult which I find rather hard to grasp. Everything is incoherent. The man who decides to have a bath but who goes to the cine-

ma. The other man who wants to keep quiet but who says things that
don't even come into his head. Another one who has an exact idea
about something but who only manages to express the opposite in
words which for him are a bad translation. No logic. Relative necessities discovered *a posteriori*, valid not from the point of view of their
exactitude, but as explanations . . . The convention of spoken language
is amply sufficient, but for ourselves alone, for our inner games and
our literature we don't need it any more.[16]

CULTIVATE YOUR OWN WILDERNESS

It would be difficult to deny that the twentieth century has been a period of exceptionally forceful competition among social paradigms. A plethora of conceptions of social reality have ripened and ultimately fallen from the contemporary tree of knowledge into a veritable cornucopia of desperate experiments and wildly hopeful fantasies, charismatic leaders, tragic swindles, some silly and some ghastly utopias, and some impressive advances. Some of these advances are already showing signs of wear and tear but have attained a degree of historical importance. Others, such as the civil rights movement, the women's movement, the mental health movement (to name a few) have left in invaluable inheritance and an example of growth and change towards healthier ways of living. Other attempts left many people with a lot of physical and emotional baggage they don't need.

Like all forms of human endeavor, poetry lives and thrives, matures and finally fades away in importance and relevance, in part, according to social conditions. As a result, as with other forms of essentially individual action, there is a dynamic relationship between the social responses to poetry and the impact of this effect on the actual practitioner's purposes and aims. The social fact, for example, that poetry has learned how to survive and even flourish almost in a vacuum, as it does in the United States, amply demonstrates the paradoxical relationship between the actual power of poetry and its apparent social reception. As illustrated by the biographies of many great poets, poetry can germinate and grow quite excellently in the arid desert of practically no response whatever. Emily Dickinson and Charles Baudelaire may serve as bright examples.

There are poets who can make the rain fall in the desert. I think of Allen Ginsberg. When he sings to hex the government, I don't hear the music of the spheres. But when he envisions, like his soulmate Walt Whitman, the individual's relationship to government, world, mind, cosmos, I wonder if everyone hasn't been transformed.

If we are to speak of the "social" as poets, I think it would be most valuable to visualize it as a largely internal entity, part reality and part fantasy, no matter what happens on television. If a poet feels the need to address the whole society, I think it would be more effective for her to do so as if she were talking directly to someone else (which partly includes, of course, talking into the void). Perhaps we ought to imagine the social as if it were a person, and in the United States, a not very well or, at times, very coherent person, and then, even as a kind of other person within that person, partly unknown to the person. To me this would approximate the "social" as it may be seen from a poet's viewpoint. In psychoanalysis this is called the superego, which I have called the "supraego" to underline those aspects of the conscience over which the individual has little power or influence. Having, in fact, very little real power to reshape society by force, at least for very long, the poet learns, like any other individual, to adapt externally. But the internal adaptation that takes place simultaneously is not like the external one, and is different in some essential way from that of the average person. The poet must learn to rebel in a certain sense internally whether or not he or she rebels externally. Without this small rebellion, staged within the self again and again, there would in fact be no poem. With groups the story is different. The fact that a very large group of people came together to protest the war in Vietnam (and I would always think of Allen Ginsberg in this context) did not alter much the overall and pervasive feeling of powerlessness among individuals in our society. So what is the power of the poet under such conditions to effect the social policy? To me the answer lies in the fact that poetry carves out a place for the social to exist in some freer way inside the individual human being. Denise Levertov once said that the "language poets" take a private space on the public beach. My response to this is that it takes a private place within for the individual to find any comfort or freedom at all on the public beach — which, in fact, is the only beach for most of us. Poetry attempts to redefine the whole of experience by confronting it with its own language, creating a self-transformative loop between language and experience, helping to externalize what is too often internally regarded by the individual as a public province.

We live in a time when much individual experience is reduced to an extreme version of social homogeneity. It is abundantly clear by now to most people in the United States that if you conform in your thoughts, you will fit in. A ready sense of humor will protect us from any sincere reaction to a departure from the usual expressions. The unconscious wish to suppress all idiosyncrasy is an obsessive trait that belongs to a primitive form of tribal self-protection. In this sense we might say that the individual has "come a long way" but the individual as group or the group as individual is still largely infantile — particularly when it doesn't get its own way with what it regards as "the stubborn individual." Under such circumstance poetry only survives in hidden forms. This means literally secret, not just esoteric or obscure, but inscrutable. In this way it protects its ageless loyalty to real experience, and real human needs. As long as the extreme social hypocrisy remains, poetry will turn to extreme means to protect itself like this, and will discover its power in guarding the ancient truths. Nothing will publicize it to the detriment of this function, no matter how energetic the broadcasting — to whatever extent the gulf between the poet and the public continues to be an externalization of the gulf between the truly valued and the unquestionably phoney. Such things cannot be changed quickly or easily, because the situation has little to do with the "social" in the reportorial sense, but more to do with the group conception of the internal human being and the group's beliefs about the conditions under which its importance is actually realized (which is in a certain sense known, but unconsciously denied, for the same reasons that so many other ideals are lost somewhere between their social acknowledgement and their actual application). Here and now the poet struggles to transgress not so much the external laws and norms which are unjust but which the group continues to declare just — as obnoxious and limiting and vicious as these can be —but the far more insidious, cancerous, and pervasive subliminally imposed internal ones. In this arena the powers and means of the poet often differ from that of other people, though they partake of the universal spirit in the individual experience, or strive to. The poet is best equipped to intelligently transgress certain extremely important, actually crucial internal entities, from a cultural viewpoint — crucial particularly to the inner needs of the productive individual within the culture. The poet's sensitivity is able to creatively transgress certain internal boundaries in order to help define their continued existence from the point of view of overall consciousness, and sometimes to even help redefine them. Sometimes poetry does the latter by helping rid the conception of the internal person of boundaries which are probably already in a rotted condition and are ready to go. It is because of this that poets can become "expert revolutionaries", though they should take care not to obsessively apply their expertise in this area, resulting from purposes that are not precisely the same as those of full-time political revolutionaries. Suffice it to say that the ordinary "peacetime" activities that each are generally attracted to are not consistently the same. The poet has special skills in creatively transgressing internal boundaries because of the wish to make a contribution to what is out there in here.

In closing I'd like to turn around that famous dictum of Gertrude Stein: we are all a found generation.

WRITING AND SPONTANEITY

From the instant of birth to the instant of death, the individual is met with the constant requirement that spontaneity be controlled. At the same time, in many interactions the individual is expected to appear spontaneous while in those very situations it is not possible for her or him to be actually feeling what is being displayed. It is no surprise that once given the opportunity to be spontaneous an individual might feel some ambivalence.

Despite many efforts to counteract this, recent events strongly point in the direction that the group is finding more and more ways to control the individual voice and mind. The recent moves against individual freedom of expression and the increasing restrictions on the National Endowment for the Arts are clear evidence of this. While it is true that there have been many victories won by means of bold experimentation in the arts, such triumphs were pyrrhic from the standpoint of freedom for writers now. While an historical procession of geniuses has generation after generation revealed an ever deeper confirmation of the individual desire for freedom, a powerful historical process of censorship has taken place to make sure that the group mind will easily hold sway over the individual mind.

What does the experimental approach imply? It points to the reality that expression itself is of enormous value because it is only through expression that anything concealed can be revealed. There is a very great temptation in the group mind to use the power of attention to give "reality" to or take "reality" away to or from a group, a cause, an idea. This lack of attention can belittle the significance of something in the eyes of the group. Conversely, the power to concentrate attention itself, through, for example, advertising, confirms the group's ability to determine which individuals will be heard.

In turn, the individual has countered such techniques of concentrating group attention by forms of experimentation. The experiments might be in physics, politics, music, medicine or poetry, but the end goal of the experiment is often to win the attention of the group towards an alternative paradigm in the way of carrying out certain activities, maintaining certain beliefs, or just feeling a certain way about something, like oneself, for example, or the group as a whole. Usually, the group's response to such experiments will be rapid and definitive. No doubt, very often the group expresses itself through an individual representative, but it will be clear to many that it is the group that is speaking. Ironically, the only way this can ever, and does ever change, is through an individual accepting the full brunt of the group's response. True, such an individual may symbolically represent a group, but this representation will never be as formal and as wholehearted as that obtained by the individual who has the explicit backing of a group or institution.

One of the most familiar expressions of spontaneity is found in structured games. Here, spontaneity consists of employing one of a specified set of moves in response to the move of another. This includes the poem as game where the King is Content and the Queen is Form, the Bishop Rhetoric and the Knight Metaphor, the Castle Imagery and the Pawns Allusions. Each moment allows for certain moves, disallowing others, taking the poem to its eventual victory or defeat. The first tournament is enacted in the mind of the poet — the later tournaments in the minds of the publishers, editors and readers — and finally in the assertions of critics, and in the end in the annals of history. Among many other things, experimental poetry arrived at the scene to propose a slightly different game. First, there would be no hierarchy of form and content, making the King and Queen of equal strength. This possibility was resisted greatly up until very recent years, shifting only slightly as structuralist and post-structuralist criticism shed some light on some earlier attempts to experiment with language (e.g., the works of Poe and Mallarmé as discussed by Roland Barthes and Jacques Lacan). The strength and quality of the old distinctions would depend on the specific writer. Some writers would not distinguish such functions at all, others would allow a remnant of this to remain, kind of like the constitutional monarchy in England.

Also, the "tournaments" (if these were to be retained) would not necessarily follow the pattern above. For example, the poet may publish her own poems and the poems of others. Also, the poet may herself become the critic of her own work. Some writers have offered theoretical models for their own work, others have renounced the primacy of earlier forms of writing. Some have even gone beyond symbolism and impressionism to demand that the reader and the writer share equally in the task of shaping meaning. Other poets have experimented with changing the way poetry expresses meanings through its visual aspects.[1] The common root in all these approaches is to allow the poet to circumvent conventions, which more and more determine what poets will say and how they will say it. Gradually, as the writer accepts full responsibility for every aspect of the poem, the authority slips away from the context and into the hands of the poet. And, at the same time, the idea of the context as moral judge is gradually replaced by the concept of the context as arbiter of forces. The old dream was one in which the game would render the forces as controllable agents; the new dream is one in which the forces emerge spontaneously as predictable agents of unpredictable change.

The re-emergence of spontaneity as a central force in creativity can be tracked in the evolution of Buddhism, for example, from the early, desire-repressing forms to the later forms like Zen Buddhism, where responsiveness and openness to feelings replace the strict controls of laws and tenets. Similarly, earlier psychological systems stressed behavioral conditioning, while more recent systems like psychoanalysis utilize free association of ideas and spontaneous expression of thoughts as methods of discovering underlying conflicts, so as to release them. However, at the same time, while such systems attempt to systematize their approaches by means of group organizations which offer course of instructions, gradually the ideal of spontaneity may be obscured by the need both to explain and to institutionalize evolving systems of practice.

2. "You can hold yourself back from the sufferings of the world, this is something you are free to do and is in accord with your nature, but perhaps precisely this holding back is the only suffering you might be able to avoid." — Kafka

Holding back here is closely related to the issue of spontaneity. Another connection is that so-called automatic writing, expressing for the sake of expressing (where the content is secondary), also called "art for art's sake," shares with Romanticism and psychoanalysis an idea of discovering through uncovering or revealing suppressed energies within the soul or psyche hopes or ideals which have been lost in the past. So that all proponents of freedom of expression find a common source of light arising from individual strivings. In this view, all individuals share the same ironic fate of a necessary lifetime struggle against an abject fusion with the strongest beliefs and wishes of the group. When an individual speaks out in opposition to this tendency, all individuals are reminded that the individual *can* speak out, while inevitably, the force of history overcomes the power of the convictions of any single individual's belief or ideals, if that is the will of the group. On the other hand, when the power of the individual is derived from the group, the group will invariably assert its power to silence the individual, even when it is announcing its efforts to curb and control this power, as in a democracy. This is why poetry which seeks the consensus of the group about its meanings and purposes is often suspect to me, though this might depend on the degree of self-reflection and irony it contains about its own meanings and purposes.

WRITING AND PERSEVERING

"God made everything out of nothing.
But the nothingness shows through."
— Paul Valéry

1. A penchant for philosophizing has gradually led me in the direction of a kind of pragmatism of heart, while my mind is left free to speculate on what it will. I say gradually only with hindsight because the onset felt sudden. One day — it seems to me now, it was very clear to me that the life of my ideas and the life of my feelings, while being clearly connected, in sure and satisfying ways, ultimately were in some basic sense completely independent of each other. I didn't think this pragmatism was ever really absent in me — deep down — but there was a period in my life when it was possible for more or less long periods of time to suspend obedience to the clear dictates of practicality. I call it a pragmatism of heart because what was really being preserved was access to a range of feelings. I has become very clear to me that when this range of feeling is more or less palpably delimited I have committed myself frequently to an action or connected group of actions which go against my perceptions of my world.

2. By continuously apprehending these feelings I ensure a sense of self. Yet at certain moments I sometimes get a glimpse of how this sense of self so intimately and immediately connects me with the many universes of other selves. With what relief I obtain to such feelings again and again. They also, by means of still another doorway lead out to all kinds of past atmospheres and textures, many small neighborhoods of forgotten experience as specific as particular tastes and smells.

3. Many of my friends and acquaintances in their writings seem to distrust this word "I". Is it seen as an insatiable monster made of mirrors, more like an inorganic substance than a breathing being? To what lengths some will go in their poems and other writing to avoid any illusion to it. Have we thus isolated it, and by so doing only contributed to its influence by means of a powerfully notable absence? To have one thing to deal with — like an ideal or set of ideals — than have to admit that one could not bear to live for very long in a selfless world — which would be like a sunless world — perhaps it's a mode of simplification. Could the absence of an abstract I be a kind of lighthouse or guidepost in itself?

4. So let this I be like a sun, or a star. It is but one among countless others, but it is also a complex world in itself. It can be forgotten that that which gives sustenance also consumes it. We too often split and divide modes of being and

even beings themselves, in order to conquer — even this is ultimately mainly a way of comprehending again that much more than there are things and people, with all knowledge and truths about them, there is nothing., just like in the inorganic universe. If we tried to compose a universe without this empty part we would be terribly crowded — and would spend more time filling than living.

5. Imagine how frustrating it would be if we always forgot that a sense of being full is quite dependent on the experience of being emptied — and that a sense of doing something is equally dependent on the sense of doing nothing. Significance pales before insignificance — and because of this we're soon back again for more. The greatest frustration of all is to forget that we live on a pendulum in every way. To forget this (the forgetting can never be absolute) amplifies the sensation of anxiety, which feels like the Earth is slipping away. All becomes hurry because closure is impossible. There is no place to stop. As Bob Dylan put it: "There must be some way outa here/Said the joker to the thief/there's too much confusion/I can't get no relief."

6. I accept comparison and laughter, love and diatribe, doubt and fecundity as my daily diet. I can't reject the bitter taste of disappointment either. To avoid this compulsively may mean paralysis. What we remember best is what we sensed was the actuality of the situation. But this doesn't nullify the other thoughts and soundings. There were innumerable small venturings that led to the knock at the door. There were moments of strangeness too before the smile of recognition. This happened so many times it became like breathing. But the first few times seemed infinitely long. Once your mind has segmented the leap into human strides the abyss has measure if still as daunting. Even chaos may get less forbidding as its features (ever changing) start announcing themselves as provoking a recognizable feeling or constellation of reactions. The giddy dizziness will finally relent and the familiar landscape will once again reveal itself. Only, one or more elements have been added with this sighting. Each round of lostnesss and foundness leaves its own set of markings on the map we make inside and constantly consult. Like any map, the more it's shared with others, the more useful it becomes. If they ignore it, don't let that stop you from proceeding on your quest. After all, it's just a map.

7. The recitation of pains gives way to the recitation of pleasures which gives way to the recitation of confusions which gives way to the recitation of assertions which gives way to the recitation of triumphs which gives way to the recitation of dangers which gives way to the recitation of discoveries which gives way to the recitation of solitudes which gives way to the recitation of judgements which gives way to the recitation of reveries which gives way to the recitation of satisfactions which gives way to the recitation of predictions which gives way to the recitation of resentments which gives way to the recitation of

memories which gives way to the recitation of personalities which gives way to the recitation of histories which gives way to the recitation of feelings which gives way to the recitation of intuitions which gives way to the recitation of visions which gives way to the recitation of experiments which gives way to the recitation of theories which gives way to the recitation of constellations which gives way to the recitation of origins which gives way to the recitation of languages which gives way to the recitation of alphabets which gives way to the recitation of elements which gives way to the recitation of characteristics which gives way to the recitation of qualities which gives way to the recitation of things which gives way to the recitation of combinations which gives way to the recitation of movements which gives way to the recitation of structures which gives way to the recitation of wholes which gives way to the recitation of fragments which gives way to the recitation of tones which gives way to the recitation of echoes which gives way to the recitation of recitations.

My poetics is concerned with a form of willful disorganization which results partly from a wish to retrieve and sustain the energy contained in the process of one idea dissolving into a set of transformations, the way a surfboard rider follows the entropic energy of a collapsing wave front. As you might expect the price I pay for the occasional sensational ride is innumerable occasions of stasis and many falls on my face and other vulnerable spots.

*

An important difference between a skilled poet and a clumsy one is that the clumsy one stops when there are no more words and the skilled one stops when there is no more beat.

*

We depend on the aesthetic to loosen the tight garments woven by necessity on the one hand and morality on the other.

*

The truth is what we must repeat. The facts are what we must accept. This is why the truth is poetic and the facts journalistic.

*

We live in a time when to systematically search out almost any form of knowledge invariably moves us in a direction of a relationship with others of a deeply compromising kind. Why this should be so is a complex question. In many areas of study it is an avoidable question to some degree. In the area of poetic creation this is an unavoidable question.

One systematic study of human beings which is considered a form of psychology I consider in part a branch of poetics — this is psychoanalysis. It is an area of poetics which concerns itself with the enduring yet in many ways incomplete connective link between people. This connective link is ensured by the human desire for others, and the human need for others. One aspect of this desire for others places the poetic impulse in jeopardy. This aspect consists of the failure to be understood. In its earliest form in childhood the failure to be understood places the possibility of a person understanding themselves in jeopardy. The poetic impulse moves in at this point to transform the wish to be understood into another register. The human — that is, the face to face encounter with incomprehension — has upset the delicately balanced system of introspective versus comparative (differentiating) and deciphering functions which make possible the infinitely complex sensor mechanisms that in turn enable individuals to guide themselves through the labyrinths of contemporary existence. The poetic impulse bypasses this flawed give-and-take by means of a fusion of communicative and receptive linguistic gestures. It is other than a mere humming to oneself and it is other than a rhapsodic singing to others. It is a way out of a deathly trap — the ultimate snare of human communication itself. Yes, a joke. But some joke.

Poetry is always out to prove that individual people can help transform, soothe, awake and not too occasionally laugh at others and themselves. One form of this is to confuse themselves (or disorient themselves) for simple out and out relief from the ultimately deadening aspects of the too many and too rational and controlled expectations of the human being. As Novalis — an 18th century visionary poet — put it: "Poetry heals the wounds inflicted by reason." And Blake: "If the fool would persist in his folly he would become wise." And Emerson: "A foolish consistency is the hobgoblin of little minds."

Our closest impulses are hard to find. We turn to group solutions, we feel challenged, warmed, encouraged, accepted, but somehow less clear. This is because the truth is composed largely of ourselves, particularly in the application. We need something for this. Something that lets us sell our dreams to each other instead of our schemes. What is interesting about this transformation is that it is constant. The professional poet takes this constant and moves it into the direction of a kind of knowledge. The blurry boundary here is between the breathing constant and the formal expression. The limit of one turns us back on the receptive regeneration of the other. The thing said becomes the gestural marker of the shared space between reader and writer. The thing said looks after those things in language that make a mind comprehensible to another mind. Something like a poetic map is drawn. "We say ourselves in syllables. . ./rising in speech we do not speak" (Wallace Stevens). There is an enchantment in drawing close enough to hear each other. Understanding is understood before anything in particular is understood. Play between two is felt before anything at all need be expressed in this play. In psychotherapy all is in place by now except the record of the event — to compare this discipline to poetry. This may come. New forms discover themselves slowly and there are healthy reasons for this. It is because we are much more in a hurry to live than we are to discover and make notes about the reasons for living. Then again, there is more than one kind of psychotherapy and there is more than one kind of poetry — as there are many ways of living a life.

Why should searching for knowledge together lead us towards the danger of compromise? The obvious reason is that people compete and people fight for control and though these fights and competitions often have very good reasons they are sometimes injurious to the open and generous sharing of knowledge — the main way it can be copiously accumulated. Such sharing obviously goes with appreciation and fighting does not go so well with accumulation, although competing can be a challenge to gathering knowledge. We move forward by means of revolutions and resolutions and we sometimes go right by what's apropos. This is because the group has resolved together to decide what is true and sometimes the united mind is wrong. Sometimes a long look back can help, but most often an individual poet will detect by means of some kind of vision-ary process the direction away from the now paralyzing misapprehension which led to less vibrant states of being. This kind of apprehension is rarely fashion-able. And we *must* have fashion.

This does not leave us with a point. Rather, it leaves us with a cloud — a blurry cloud of thought. We're back where we were when the impulse brought us here. There is a common ground in such shared confusion which may be bet-ter than shared delusion. A shared delusion can result from the need for an explanation or a guiding principle or person when any one of these "solutions" may be more destructive than instructive or constructive. In government this can show itself in providing a rationale for choosing expediency over good judgement. In psychoanalysis and social work such shared delusion may be implicit when procedures are blindly followed as a clinician's shield against an analysand's overwhelming anxiety and chaotic behavior. Such defensiveness often grows out of a fear of loss of control which is frequently the underlying motivation for what psychoanalysis terms "resistance": the unconscious reluc-tance to search further. In art, in poetry and other forms of writing such difficul-ties usually announce their presence by the notorious "writer's block" — or in strong impulses to find avenues of escape, such as certain kinds of counterpro-ductive and masochistic behavior, or the artist's tendency to anxiously rush into the completion of a specific work or group of works.

Not long ago I ransacked the meager writings of one of my favorite com-posers, Claude Debussy, in an effort to discover his artistic "secret", particularly the ability of his work to sustain its aura despite many listenings. What I found was this:

Time spent carefully creating the atmosphere in which a work of art must move is never wasted. As I see it, one must never be in a hurry to write things down. One must allow the complex play of ideas free rein: how it works is a mystery and we too often interfere with it by being impatient — which comes from being too materialistic, even cowardly, though we don't like to admit it.[1]

You put such strong pressure on your ideas that they no longer dare present themselves to you, they're so afraid of not being dressed in a way you'd approve of. You don't let yourself go enough and in particular you don't seem to allow enough play to that mysterious force which guides us towards the true expression of a feeling, whereas dedicated, single-minded searching only weakens it.[2]

AFTERMATH: EPILOGUE

9/8/86

Everyone must have a night world and a day world. And often, this day world is as afraid of unleashed work, as the night one is of unleashed love.

2/7/87

The years are not numbers, they're more like letters spelling out a word.

2/15/87

When you know what you want, look at the obstacles as annoyances, not as disappointments.

Time is still — it's our hands that move.

The question of immensity is partly one of visualization.

Since fantasies are also current actualities, time can be visualized as a loop, rather than an arrow, as a tide, rather than a stream.

3/22/87

Again, the idea that writing is an invention for the hand and another sense, like the violin or a comb.

4/11/87

The smoothest running machine has a hairy part that allows for leaks to and from a proximate surround.

5/22/87

The discontinuity of thought is assured by the role fantasy and dreams play in it.

We might see what the metaphysicians were searching for at the antipodes of the form for all-that-there-is.

5/28/87

We don't have knowledge, we wear it. Is this because of the tight relationship between knowing and believing?

6/14/87

The cutting edge of narrative often turns to blood and is fascinated by monsters.

7/4/87

A "private language" or "obscure poetry" or "automatic writing" are ways of describing the products of the writer holding to the value that it is as important to give expression to something in order to know what it is, than it is to know what it is in order to give expression to it. "Free speech," "free association," "private language": they just go together.

8/10/87

The lightest of things — like insects, like birds, like joy — may be easily crushed. The heaviest things — stones, sorrows — these stay, and tend to hold their shape.

The poem may occur in a place which is greatly dissimilar from the world made apparent to the senses. But wherever it is, one fine day there or nearby you will meet its poet.

8/10/87

Experience only apparently repeats itself. Because it often seems to, we can easily forget how fortunate we were that things came together the way they did. No doubt fate did this, but it also took a tremendous effort of will — or so it seemed — not to toss it all into the air, moments before, in total frustration.

10/25/87

The arts flatter people by making the improbable seem easy to attain — and the easy impossible to do.

10/31/87

Sometimes, close-up, a piece of writing, a solution to the puzzle, seems all wrong. Yet somewhere someone touches me and I touch back.

11/7/87

Deciding is always the hardest part of any action.

11/14/87

Lautreamont (*Poesies*): "The science I undertake is a science distinct from poetry. I do not sing of the latter. I strive to discover its source."

11/15/87

Heraclitus, Fragment CXXV: "The fairest order in the world is a heap of random sweepings."

11/19/87

Light hurts the eyes in a gloomy age.

11/25/87

Dexterity replaces depth now because complexity demands speed rather than closeness of fit. As a result there are more pleasures and pain is deep but swift.

12/12/87

The pathos of life lies in the disparity between the specific thing we are focused on and the fact of life itself.

12/27/87

Tristan Tzara: "look at the clock which becomes language."

12/29/87

Poetry: A language without a homeland.

1/1/88 - 2/13/88

An inner measure of things taken as a palpable surface is engraved into a person's self by the constant pressures of experience. The mind has a chance of staying ahead of this — laboring to clean its own slate — but the disparity is hard on balance.

*

The closer you look into a mirror, the more you see your own face. Someone else is exactly what you won't find there.

*

Hold a few things in place and watch where the change occurs. Order is one kind of illusion very useful for steadying the structure.

*

The abandoned journey began with a single step.

*

To love is to return.

*

Not a form of address, but a language. The difference between a greeting and a truth.

*

In these days more often than not poems are slaps. And we deserve it. Deserve what?

*

Be prepared to make sacrifices, large and small, in order to take control of your life. But don't be in such a hurry.

*

Time took us apart. Why? Time put us together.

*

Style is as much a question of undress as it is of dress. Letting down my guard, I imagined saying things to people I would never allow myself to say in everyday life. In this fantasy, I usually pause for a moment of intense satisfaction. It is life, not the imagination, which is oblique and mysterious.

*

The source of humor in the tolerance and recognition of paradox and contradiction. Playful "attack" sometimes necessary for learning.

*

Sense organs are also sexual organs.

*

I hid my work — and hence my ideas — the way a parent protects a child. But then the child became isolated.

*

Every freedom has its price. But this is true because price is a parasite that feeds on anything. Freedom protects itself in its constant attention in watching for an opening.

*

Freedom is sometimes evasive — right. But this is in the spirit of advancing. While evasion contains a kind of freedom, it is not generative of freedom. Freedom raises, so it scares.

*

Structure is strong. This is why it sometimes seems beautiful. But the beauty is not in the structure. It is in the particularity.

*

Where am I going? Probably back to where all things came from. Why did I come? The tendency for things to come together.

*

Senses play with each other, like children, like birds.

*

People attach themselves to things and to ideas. Often the two conflict. But both commitments are strong.

*

The power of human tenacity is inestimable. Is this the most prominent simi- larity — in personality — to our ancestors — the apes?

*

Why do writers imagine that readers have no sense of touch in their eyes? Reading is all Braille.

*

Reader and writer — little faith in each other. Both fear betrayal — but the reader more, even though the writer takes most of the risk.

*

The final thought of thought is freedom from thought.

*

Coming apart at the seems: "What is = what I did."

*

Thoughts are an intrusion, but not that much of an intrusion. What is a true invasion is a misperception, a falsehood, a lie.

*

Even obscurity has properties.

*

Language gives form to the impact the world has on our inner measure of it.

*

Things that really come before come after too.

*

Having a thought is like cooking an egg. The precision is all in the cracking.

*

Everything has its eye.

*

In order to do a different kind of thinking, we learn to do a new kind of writing — the *relationship* produces what is new, like a new kind of speaking. Art combines, where science atomizes.

*

If you want to keep it for yourself, keep it to yourself. Anything revealed is public property.

*

Through the mind of the critic to the heart of the poet — and vice versa.

*

"The poet is pushed to the margin" (Wim Wenders, *Wings of Desire*). Often by other poets, I might add.

*

If you want to speak, ride the rapids of sarcasm.

*

Time sings us, plays us. In revery we feel the stillness inside all the speed, glimpse how fast we must move in this social world, just to keep up with our "selves." Desire and expectation, pulsing, pulsing. Winnicott: false and true selves.

*

Time is sub-rosa ("the rose in ancient times was an emblem of silence.")

*

Now I see why I always mistyped "tiies" for "times."

*

A misplaced action corresponds to a misplaced thought.

*

"Missing" the present.

*

Eternal refrain of a child: "say it again."

*

Everything has its I.

*

Coagulation, struggle, dissolution, repeat.

*

As soon as something exists, it's complicated. Things quickly acquire other dimensions, if only because of what they are close to.

*

Movement awakens life.

*

"Seek and ye shall find." But what you find is how to find.

*

An interesting effect of John Cage's work is that it freed me of John Cage's "work." This is a profound philosophical effect and the music is no less memorable.

*

Art is finding, science is keeping, work is reaping.

*

To be decorous is not to be formalistic. The first may simply be showing sensitivity to a formal context. The second creates a context.

*

In everyday practice, truths are detected by apprehending cadences. These are confirmed by a kind of subliminal sounding that employs aspects of vision and touch.

*

Charm furthers propagation.

*

They can interrupt or stop anything but true celebration. Celebration, cerebration. Could this have been the first act of mental freedom?

*

Pierce the membrane between philosophy and poetry and something starts to leak, then flow.

*

Happiness is always "conventional."

*

Irritation: surplus stimulation.

*

Wisdom: does it consist of little more than accepting how long it takes for something to actually "happen"? If satisfaction is the measure this is easy to see.

*

Perfection is a kind of surface. Wholeness must be bounded by a shell or skin. To be a unit is to have an outside and an inside.

*

Place your bets, then laugh. And the game comes to an end so soon!

*

In case you might forget, exaggerate.

*

Adhering to the world by means of glue, ideas are useful mainly when they're wet. But the dry remains fascinate.

*

Reality is like a sea.

*

The world contains many thoughts and few images.

2/13/88

The middle state between the permanent establishment of an inner object and its earlier, rudimentary form within the ego is reflected in the child's game "hide and go seek." This is an attempt to sublimate into playful excitement the same sort of anxiety that emerges when an adult loses or misplaces something important, or feels threatened by the absence of a person or place. Freud observed that the whole attitude of a worried person resembles that of someone struggling to remember something. This something (a repressed thought) is now the faded image of the missing object. The loss of something stimulates a memory which in turn stimulates anxiety. This memory is the memory of not yet being able to remember.

7/11/88

In order to live at the pitch of contemporary life, we acquire the ability to forgo the intervals of time that are actually needed to consolidate and make part of ourselves what we have already experienced. Because of the multiplicity of life's possibilities and demands there is little time for this consolidation. Thus we gradually harden ourselves to accommodate reality and even further forget what it is like to imagine really digesting something.

7/13/88

"Time out of time."

*

The more I am heard, the more I must resort to silence to be heard. The quicker I go, the more stealthily I must move.

*

What you are looking for, accept only that, even if you have to collect it in very small amounts over long periods of time.

7/14/88

The imagination forthrightly encountered can never betray and will always reveal. For this encounter to be open internally, however, is as difficult, and consequently as rare, as in external encounters.

*

The art of creating occasions for writing eventually gets tied into the entire system of values a writer lives by.

7/18/88

Life presents itself to us, all at once, at all times, in its entirety.

8/28/88

The literary garden (or jungle) seems to grow best under conditions of excess, whether these are the personal excesses of an author, excessive zeal for a belief, personality, or group of personalities, for the act of literary creation itself, or the excesses of society during a certain period.

The conditions of a literary composition must correspond to a world, not necessarily according to the way the everyday world organizes itself, but it must correspond to what is most frequently encountered about this world, that is, the richness and variety not only of disparate things, but the variations among simultaneously occurring types of experience. So various are these transformations in a world, that the same variety which stuns in its lushness, also overwhelms in its manifestations of change. But all this is usually discernible only under literary conditions that are mostly free of an author's intention to persuade or dissuade by means of moral example.

9/4/88

Impossible to write a kind of poetry in which the unconscious aim is to create (reveal) a code that almost can't be cracked (analogue to the enigmatic nature of reality itself) and to also have the pleasure of seeing almost every aspect be constantly governable. In this sense my approach to writing (and the one I seem to most often enjoy in the writing of others) contains an important anarchic aspect, a "jungle" or "jumble'" or "mumbo-jumbo" that permits things to thrive together unnoticed, or could utter involuntarily from its throat a garbled kind of truth — garbled necessarily because of the resistances which arise in the uncovering of any mystery. This truth is not a deduction, reduction or introduction — it is the description of life which has the smell of life — a most venerable scratch 'n sniff. But the same element which creates this palpably funky aspect also threatens to cause to be said that which seemed unspeakable in any other way.

*

The charm of certain writers, and artists, may consist more in their lifelong commitment to a certain way of understanding, whose works — and lives — exemplify a certain perspective in living. Their lives consist of a kind of investigation — private investigation — private "I's" that constantly seem to continue along their own way, not oblivious to the world but of necessity tangent to it at times. Learning about — and, even more, knowing such a person — is often experienced as an inspiration. At one point I experienced this in relation to the writings of Freud, at another to Paul Valéry's.

*

Ideas accumulate one at a time. A constantly disruptive drive that persists in the imagination is the endless search for a completed underlying frame or structure. But the discovery of this structure is equal in its importance to the attainment of the uncrackable code: one opens us to the world, the other closes us against the world to acquire or to keep something within. The code contains a dare or a risk. Can it attract enough memory to itself to be read again, and yet, not contain such specificity that it can be remembered at a glance? A good poem, like a healthy body, wants to be touched repeatedly, at intervals, but also, like a person, wants to retain its identity and not merge with the world it wants to embrace and be embraced by. In order for a poem to need to be read more than once it must offer tempting glimpses of a world which, in everyday life, would otherwise remain largely invisible. To "describe" the world as it is given, summarily, is to provide an inventory, not a poem. A poem which is little more than an ordinarily spoken, or even sung, summation of everyday life experience, however detailed, however epiphanous or rapturous, witty or insightful, will rarely be read more than once because it cannot evoke more upon rereading other than the constant repeating of the days. No one needs another wallet-sized snapshot of life to add to the album of similar snapshots. We need poems that accumulate us, not that we accumulate.

*

Crowds — someone on the outskirts of the crowd — escaping? (Benjamin)

9/12/88

Things resist manipulation and usually respond better to a frank and solid grasp.

9/14/88

A poetics that allows a poem to begin with any word or with no words at all. This is no simple democracy of experience or call for "automatic writing." This is the complete abandonment of any kind of privileged experience. Chance need not play the role of leveller, a kind of yardstick to compare one kind of observation with another. That there isn't (won't be for long) one absolute means of measure or comparison leads not to a benign or complacent recognition of the relativism of values, but to a conceptual glimpse into the intrinsic ferment underlying reality. A recognition, sometimes ecstatic, sometimes terrifying, sometimes simply dreary, that actuality *is* revolution, or *actuality* is revolution.

9/20/88

The poetry of murder helped instigate the murder of poetry.

Looking for the root, I forgot the sun.

10/27/88

Specific awareness of any state of mind constitutes a kind of certainty.

*

Publishing writing is a dare, a way of initiating struggle at a boundary. Writing consolidates reading, reading generates a kind of vacuum, a kind of frustrated silence. Reading demands expression, writing demands reception.

10/28/88

Consciousness, that master poet, never forgets that final touch, even when the heart itself does.

10/29/88

You come to the delicate portion, which is the center of the machine. You get there by means of feeling your way, because your eyes are no good to you there. Your feelers fly in the air. You touch the delicate part with your feelings-feelers, and the whole machine moves.

12/8/88

Then I realized that I myself was history going backwards — I saw the improbability of every event as wondrous in itself, and suggestive of times past and those to come.

2/8/89

False hope is the final boundary, the lonely, lovely shore of all relationships — and there is a glowing sunset of such sad times.

3/16/89

It is reasonable to conclude that it is not reasonable to conclude.

3/22/89

Poetry encourages us to say things aloud — or think them aloud — an action which tends to jog memories.

4/21/89

Beware, dear philosopher — behind the ghost of every argument is the ghost of a person come to haunt you.

*

Don't think of the gallows at the beach — think of the beach at the gallows.

6/19/89

The book itself is the fiction.

7/4/89

Small occurrences which are trifling in the macro world, but are momentous in the micro world. Satie: the child's march. Self-importance of those "little men."

7/14/89

The toy you can't forget is now a tyrant.

*

Books are having an evolution just like primates. First they have spines of their own — much later they have minds of their own.

*

Don't forget, the expert chiseler knows how to get you to like giving it over.

9/2/89

Being unable to wait is what brings about the embarrassing numbers. The world, via dissolution, returns with death to oppose this conception of reality, itself a victim of objectivity, which, like subjectivity, is temporary. Though I voluntarily subscribe to these conditions, I can claim this appropriation of my perceptions for the world's purposes in defining itself as an injury.

*

Objectivity / touch / grasp

Subjectivity / sleep / encompassment

12/10/89

The soul of a nation is composed of its poets. Individuals can't see their souls either.

12/24/89

To be presented with wise thoughts causes me to feel soothed in the short run — and more vigilant in the long run.

One thing leads to another. For something not to lead to something else probably means that it wasn't really something at all — it was probably a pseudothing.

12/30/89

Coincidences force themselves upon us at times when we are most in need of seeing the connections between events, when a good part of rationality consists of our ability to keep such connections in the background so as to continue to make interpretations along the lines of conventional expectations.

1/13/90

It seemed as if because we had rid ourselves of the efficacy of the concept of gods we had also rid ourselves of the concept of evil forces. Now we have a concept of evil as a disease which consists of biographical examples of evil, such as case histories and the histories of despots. These examples replace the function of myths in other times. But now to imagine dark forces everywhere can no longer be considered hysteria. There are often no names for what we fear and hate, except for our biases. This situation considerably supports many tragic and some unforgivable silences.

1/19/90

The art work as processional. Roman Catholics have a ritual called a "novena" which consists of a contemplative walking around the church from depiction to depiction of Jesus Christ's life.

1/21/90

You point the mind in a certain direction while remaining with the most recent observation. This parallax offers a focal point for change. It is the cognitive equivalent of setting the sails.

Understanding brings conviction. Conviction brings change.

1/26/90

Goethe: "never hurry, never rest."

Power inevitably attracts the attention of the powerful.

2/3/90

Failure to understand it made it appear unlikely.

2/21/90

Authorship and the myth of the voice out of nowhere.

Isn't it true? In a certain sense I am your friend to the extent I am your quirk.

3/1/90

"But if you can't joke, you can't talk." (Charles Bernstein — remark overheard in conversation)

3/4/90

It is very possible that as human beings we are accumulating illusions faster than we are shedding them, despite our well-intentioned efforts to reverse this process.

Somewhere between the need to connect and the wish to express, language missteps and compromises. This compromise gradually undermines the initial impulse to transcend the self. At all levels we more or less misjudge how we might connect with each other in order to protect ourselves. Language is the document of this frustration and dissatisfaction. Poetry is the written result of the attempt to overcome this dilemma.

3/7/90

Most works could probably consist of one sentence. But since we're never patient enough to think of most of the implications of even one sentence, the author offers hundreds or thousands seducing and flattering the reader into hanging around almost as long as it would take to fully understand the one.

*

Movement: — centrality of movement in physical reality focusses attention on those aspects of experience that occupy duration. But what of those aspects of actuality that do not have as their most outstanding aspect a "spread" in duration? These are the things we take for granted. Aspects of reality are like a shell game that redirects our attention away from the silent, uneventful world of the given, into the sparkling, shifting world of eventful occurrences.

4/1/90

Completeness vs. incompleteness: —

If I am incomplete, you don't ask me to step forward.

If I am complete, I need not step forward.

4/21/90

As soon as we remove our fingers from the keys of one set of worries, a new set suggests itself to us in a new key.

For space, the infinite. For mind, the if-in-it(e).

5/17/90

Each age benefits from the accomplishments of all the previous ages, as well as inheriting the results of the shortcomings. With such a large inheritance, why worry? The individual becomes the bored and careless driver of a conveyance the functions of which each has much need and the mechanisms of which each has little knowledge. So the connections between the driver and the machine grow untrustworthy.

6/24/90

There is a moral to every thought just as there is a moral to very tale.

Thought itself is the fiction.

6/28/90

Art is composed of touches. This is what the amateur has difficulty understanding. Once the scaffolding has been built — then touches.

Doing things. In any case, they will be done one at a time. Thinking about the number makes a person rush. Numbers, mathematics, calendars, money — all the things that remain to be done.

7/4/90

Democritus of Abdera:

116. I came to Athens and no one knew me.

8/1/90

"Looking for" themes, narratives, anecdotes, it's all grown so wearisome. 19th Century charms played and replayed, like wonderful old tunes. This is outside my experience.

These books are like stereopticons, those old gadgets that held two slides, which the binoculars turned into one with an illusion of depth.

9/19/90

"I imagine that when we reach the boundaries of things set for us, or even before we reach them, we can see into the infinite, just as on the surface of the earth we gaze out into immeasurable space." (Lichtenberg — *Aphorisms*)

9/29/90

Insofar as we are poets, we are Baudelaire.

Leave the germ of an idea as a germ. That you see it as "small" is a result of perspective.

More, or longer?

10/18/90

We all rise to greet the poet
This morning the poet is the Sun
Last night's poet was the Moon
The Moon which sung to the Sea.
In between, the dream.

11/23/90

"I can think of no state so unsupportable and dreadful, as to have the soul vivid and afflicted, without means to declare itself." (Montaigne)

1/8/91

The self is enhanced when life gets what it wants from us; identity is enhanced when we get what we want from life.

For most poets, life appears as a ferment.

1/22/91

Things on a certain tiny scale can come alive in the viscous boundary between two larger realities. These small things grow, seeds in specks of earth or water, to become living beings in a world of their own.

2/21/91

The god of bad luck tends to get sleepy. This is why it's probably best to be quiet about good luck. As soon as that old creep gets wind that any luck is happening at all, he starts to feel obliged to work and wakes up.

2/25/91

A truth does not function like a fact but like a force. The antithesis of a truth is not an untruth but someone else's truth.

3/19/91

Nothing can change your fate. Yet if reality conspires to find a way to tell you something — listen.

4/30/91

The hardest question to answer truthfully is, "How are you?" The only defense is a lie, so this question is also the greatest producer of liars.

5/16/91

A poem needs a mother and a father.

5/31/91

Sooner or later, even death must die.

6/28/91

The greatest feats of all usually result from someone relying completely on a few basic convictions.

8/20/91

"If one perceives art as anything other than strange, one does not perceive it at all." (Theodore Adorno)

8/22/91

An odd thing about human beings is that they cannot truly rest until they've done everything they can.

9/4/91

Luck and love may have something in common — they benefit from and elicit unique forms of devotion.

9/14/91

The narcissist always needs to be placed on a pedestal. You are the pedestal.

9/24/91

There is a naive conception of growth that is identified as magic.

9/30/91

Moment after moment, let each thing have its place.

10/10/91

Do it the wrong way first, but do it.

10/19/91

With all that has been said, still all has not been said.

11/24/91

If you are going to listen that closely, you had better learn how not to hear sometimes.

12/1/91

The problem still exists — and so does the solution. Think of all the hard work that goes into keeping the two separate.

Only when you give yourself over to the dream (thought, idea) does it fully open itself to you. But then you are no longer the you that gave yourself. This is why you hesitate.

12/7/91

Life changed my life.

12/20/91

Easier to live with a margin of error, than a margin of terror.

12/29/91

Luck is faith.

1/11/92

If you don't succeed the first time, show some gratitude you survived at all.

1/30/92

Love and knowledge accumulate. Time and actions don't.

1/30/92

Me too.

Love lasts longest. This may be why it has such a hand in the beginnings of things. Did it, then, have a hand in the beginning of everything?

3/8/92

There's always that moment when the knife must cut close to the hand.

4/1/92

The daily panacea: I don't remember — and — it doesn't matter.

4/2/92

What is more foregrounded — the facts or the feelings about the event?

4/4/92

Most things we do in order to forget about them. These things should not be thought about too much.

4/5/92

I'd like to say how discouraged and disappointed I feel, but discreetly, I don't; I'd like to say how proud I am that nonetheless I push on, but modestly I won't. Then the two cancel each other out.

4/6/92

You thought the motivations determined the actions, but maybe it was the other way around.

4/7/92

Slaves 'r us.

4/9/92

A firm resolution never needs a reminder.

4/12/92

In definition "maybe" means "it is possible." In everyday use "maybe" usually is taken to mean "It is probable." Does this change signify an erosion of the will?

4/17/92

The form we give to our thoughts bears a close resemblance to the shape we give to our lives.

Look at the person you most intensely dislike and find a mirror.

The feeling of anger is a signal — the oral expression of anger is a result of impatience, which usually stems from anxiety and fear.

4/19/92

Genius — someone who actually gives a shit.

The reader's deep, consoling sigh . . .

Psychoanalysis: face to face reading.

4/23/92

Frequent despondancy: reverie stolen from time reserved for duties.

4/29/92

Lie to yourself frequently and many will deceive you. Talk to yourself honestly and most will receive you.

5/27/92

In order to proceed, you must go in more than one direction. What you want to court, must court you.

5/31/92

More and more I see the closeness of "it" and "if."

Those that are not free may think their chains can keep them free.

When one thing counts for too much, everything else means nothing.

The thought, the talk, the written word — a glance ashore as we swim on.

6/1/92

The furor is over, all is in balance, and soon the current catches me again.

6/8/92

There is only one secret to life and it is known to every child: enjoy it!

6/10/92

Something goes wrong — but frequently this experience points to the door to another way of doing things. Maybe what you needed was behind this door.

7/4/92

On the surface level time is measured by minutes, hours and days. On deeper levels it is measured by intentions.

NOTES

WRITING AND SELF-DISCLOSURE

1. Kilton Stewart, *Pygmies and Dream Giants* (New York, NY: Harper and Row, 1975), p. 278.

WRITING, IDENTITY, AND THE SELF

1. Charles Bernstein, "Writing and Method," an essay written in conjunction with a series on "Poetry and Philosophy" he conducted with Edmund Leites at the St. Mark's Poetry Project, New York City, February 1981, in *Content's Dream* (Los Angeles: Sun and Moon Press, 1986).

2. Charles Bernstein and Bruce Andrews, "Pacifica Interview on Politics" *L=A=N=G=U=A=G=E*, Supplement No. 3 (October 1981).

3. Charles Bernstein, "Three or Four Things I Know About Him" *A Hundred Posters*, No. 26 (February 1978), ed. Alan Davies. Republished *L=A=N=G=U=A=G=E*, Supplement No. 3, (October 1981).

4. Charles Bernstein, "The Taste Is What Counts" in *Poetic Justice* (Baltimore, Maryland: Pod Books, 1979), p. 41.

5. Heinz Kohut, *The Restoration of the Self* (New York: International Universities Press, 1977), p. 286.

6. Charles Bernstein, "Out Of This Inside" in *Poetic Justice*. op. cit., pp. 28-29.

7. "The Taste Is What Counts", ibid, pp. 47.

8. ibid, pp. 47-48.

9. ibid, p. 46.

10. ibid, p. 47.

TOWARDS AN EXPERIENTIAL SYNTAX

1. "A Note Upon the 'Mystic Writing Pad,'" in Sigmund Freud: *Collected Papers*, vol. 5, ed. James Strachey (New York: Basic Books, 1959), p. 180.

2. See "Narration in the Psychoanalytic Dialogue," by Roy Schafer, in *On Narrative*, ed. W. J. T. Mitchell (Chicago: University of Chicago Press, 1981), pp. 25-50.

3. Donald P. Spence, *Narrative Truth and Historical Truth* (New York: W. W. Norton & Co., 1982), p. 270.

4. Ron Silliman, "Migratory Meaning: The Parsimony Principle in the Poem" *Poetics Journal* 2 (September 1982), p. 32.

5. See Robert Smithson, "A Museum of Language in the Vicinity of Art," in *The Writings of Robert Smithson* (New York: NYU Press, 1979), p. 67.

6. Barrett Watten, "Note," in *L=A=N=G=U=A=G=E* 2 (April 1978), p. 4.

7. Heinz Kohut, *Restoration of the Self* (New York: International Universities Press, 1977), p. 279.

8. Erving Goffman, *Frame Analysis* (New York: Harper and Row, 1974).

9. Edward M. MacKinnon, *Scientific Explanation and Atomic Physics* (Chicago: University of Chicago Press, 1982), p. 363-67.

10. Werner Heisenberg, *Physics and Philosophy* (New York: Harper and Row, 1958).

11. Georg Schmidt and Robert Schenk, eds., *Kunst und Naturform* (Basel: Basilius Press, 1958), pp. 122-23.

12. Banesh Hoffman, *Albert Einstein: Creator and Rebel* (New York: New American Library, 1972), p. 255.

13. See Harold Searles, *The Non-Human Environment: In Normal Development and Schizophrenia* (New York: International University Press, 1960).

14. See Gerald Holton and Yehuda Elkana, Eds., *Albert Einstein: Historial and Cultural Perspectives* (Princeton: Princeton University Press, 1982).
   "Before Einstein, however, no one had combined visual thinking so effectively with the thought-experiment, that is, an experiment capable of being performed in the mind." In Arthur I. Miller "The Special Relativity Theory: Einstein's Response to the Physics of 1905", p. 15.

15. Gilles Deleuze and Felix Guattari, *On the Line*, trans. John Johnston (New York: Semiotext(e), 1983).

16. George Kubler, *The Shape of Time* (New Haven: Yale University Press, 1962).

17. "Recommendations for Physicians on the Psycho-Analytic Method of Treatment," in Sigmund Freud: *Collected Papers*, 2:324.

18. Sigmund Freud, *The Interpretation of Dreams*, ed. James Strachey (New York: Avon Books ed. of the Standard Edition), p. 135.

19. Jacques Lacan, *Ecrits: A Selection* (New York: Norton & Co., 1977), p. 22.

20. Alan Davies and Nick Piombino, "The Indeterminate Interval: From History to Blur," in *Open Letter/L=A=N=G=U=A=G=E*.

21. Fred Ritchin, "Photography's New Bag of Tricks," *New York Times Magazine* (4 November 1984): "'In ten years we will be able to bring Clark Gable back and put him in a new show,' predicts John D. Goodell, a consultant on computer graphics for motion pictures and education. Despite the difficulties of replicating by computer natural substances like hair and skin, many researchers are tantalized by the goal of mathematically creating a realistic human image. (The legal ramifications of 'reviving' a dead movie star or any other personality might turn out to be problematic.). . . In the not too distant future, realistic-looking images will probably have to be labeled, like words, as either fiction or non-fiction, because it may be impossible to tell them apart. We may have to rely on the image-maker, and not the image, to tell us into which category certain pictures fall. . . . Photography has long been thought of as a generally trustworthy unbiased transcriber of reality, easily understood and incredibly powerful. . . . The eventual introduction of simulation techniques — with people and things realistically shown that may not have existed before, or at least not as depicted — combined with the computer's sophisticated retouching techniques, may well alter society's reliance on photograph as a documentary tool" (48-54).

CURRENTS OF ATTENTION IN THE POETIC PROCESS

* (epigraph) Frances Ponge, *The Power of Language*, translated by Serge Gavronsky (Berkeley: University of California Press, 1979), p.47.

1. *Webster's New Twentieth Century Dictionary*, Second Edition (Collins World, 1975), p. 91.
2. Jurgen Habermas, *Knowledge and Human Interests*, trans. Jeremy J. Shapiro (Boston: Beacon Press, 1971).

3. André Breton, *Manifestoes of Surrealism*, trans. Richard Seaver and Helen R. Lane (Ann Arbor: University of Michigan Press, 1974), p. 125.

4. Benjamin Fielding, Ed.D., "Focussing in Dynamic Short Term Therapy," *Colloquium* (Volume 2, Number 1, June 1979), p. 64.

5. Werner Heisenberg, *Physics and Philosophy* (New York: Harper Torchbook, 1962).

6. Albert Einstein, *Ideas and Opinions* (New York: Bonanza Books, 1954), pps. 25-26.

7. Sigmund Freud, *The Interpretation of Dreams* (Avon Edition of Standard Edition, 1965, Chapter 7, Part B), p. 573.

8. Albert Einstein, *Historical and Cultural Perspectives*, ed. Gerald Holton and Yehuda Elkana (Princeton: Princeton University Press, 1982), p. 154.

9. Roland Barthes, *Empire of Signs*, trans. Richard Howard (New York: Hill and Wang, 1982).

10. Jacques Derrida, *Of Grammatology*, trans. G. C. Spivak (Baltimore: The Johns Hopkins University Press, 1976), p. 76.

11. Albert Einstein, *Relativity, The Special and the General Theory* (New York: Crown Publishers, 1961), p. 140.

12. Sigmund Freud, *The Interpretation of Dreams*, op. cit., p. 575.

13. Sigmund Freud, *Collected Papers*, Volume IV (New York: Basic Books Edition of Standard Edition, 1959), p. 184.

14. Rainer Maria Rilke, *Where Silence Reigns*, trans. G. Craig Houston (New York: New Directions, 1978), p. 54 (originally published as "Primal Sounds," 1919), translated by C. Craig Houston.

15. ibid., pp. 53-54.

16. ibid., p. 55.

17. C.f. above, p. 28. The sign constantly displays its maddening ability to outwit its supposed 'associated' thought, and as its creator seizes on the reminiscence of its genesis, the acausal connecting process of association determines the actual signification. These meanings ordinarily are interpreted in intervallic measures or 'beats' of time.

18. Barrett Watten, *Total Syntax* (Carbondale: Southern Illinois University Press, 1985), p. 65.

19. Albert Einstein, *Historical and Cultural Perspectives*. op. cit., p. 154.

20. Sigmund Freud, *The Interpretation of Dreams*, op. cit., p. 574, quoted in Jacques Derrida, *Writing and Difference* (Chicago: The University of Chicago Press, 1978), p. 216.

21. Charles Bernstein, "Stray Straws and Straw Men," *Open Letter*, ed. Steve McCaffery, Third Series, No. 7, Summer 1977, p. 96.

22. Roman Jakobson and Krystyna Pomorska, *Dialogues* (Cambridge: The MIT Press, 1983), p. 71: "Over the centuries, the science of language has more than once addressed the question of ellipsis which manifests itself at difference verbal levels: sounds, syntax, and narration. It should be noted that for the most part these questions have been worked out only episodically and fragmentarily. A technique which today receives even less consideration is that of elliptical perception, by which the listener fills in (again on all linguistic levels) whatever has been omitted by him as speaker. We have also failed to appreciate properly the subjective attitude of the hearer who creatively fills in elliptic gaps."

SUBJECT TO CHANGE

1. Tina Darragh, "PROCEDURE" in *The L=A=N=G=U=A=G=E Book*, ed. Bruce Andrews and Charles Bernstein (Southern Illinois University Press, 1984), p. 107-108.

2. Wallace Stevens, *The Collected Poems of Wallace Stevens* (New York: Knopf, 1954), p. 350.

3. Ibid., p. 486.

4. Stéphane Mallarmé, "L'Après-Midi D'une Faune", my own translation adapted from that of David Paul, *Poison and Vision* (New York: Vintage Books, 1974), p. 161.

5. Francis Ponge, "Reading The Sun On Radio," in *The Power of Language*, trans. Serge Gavronsky (Berkeley: University of California Press, 1979), p. 97.

6. Wallace Stevens, *The Necessary Angel* (New York: Random House, 1951), p. 33.

7. K.C. Cole, *Sympathetic Vibrations: Reflections of Physics as a Way of Life* (New York: Bantam, 1985), p.59.

8. ibid., p. 52, p. 57.

9. Erving Goffman, *Frame Analysis* (New York: Harper and Row, 1974).

10. Ron Silliman, *Paradise* (Providence: Burning Deck, 1985), p. 40.

11. Charles Bernstein, *Senses of Responsibility* (Berkeley: Tuumba Press [Tuumba 20], 1979), p. 1-2.

12. Jackson Mac Low, "Language-Centered" in *L=A=N=G=U=A=G=E*, Volume 4, edited by Bruce Andrews and Charles Bernstein (Open Letter, Fifth Series, No. 1) p. 26. Virtually all of Mac Low's superb "non-intensional" poetry could illustrate the type of writing described as perceiver-centered.

13. K.C. Cole, op. cit., p. 211 (quoting Niels Bohr).

14. Walter Benjamin, quoted in "(In)citations/(Ex)positions" by Didier Cahen, *Banana Split*, Number 14.

15. Bruce Andrews, "Jeopardy", in *Wobbling* (New York: Roof Books, 1981), p. 90.

16. Tristan Tzara, *Seven Dada Manifestos and Lampisteries*, trans. Barbara Wright (New York: Riverrun Press, 1984), p. 111.

WRITING AND SPONTANEITY

1. The best example of a completely successful poetic improvisation of the purest visual type that I can think of is *Marquee* by Ray DiPalma (and a related earlier work *The Sargasso Transcries* (*Marquee* was published by Asylum's Press, 1977, *The Sargasso Transcries* by X Editions, 1974). This work, which is the exact inverse of conventional written language — neither recreates, nor deconstructs experience, it provokes it by a kind of metrical and lettristic prompting. This work may contain within it a foundation for the poetic discovery of the precise experiential locale where shape becomes sound. It seems to me desperately important that the connection between visual imagining and linguistic imagining be rediscovered for our period. It is very possible that this could only be done improvisationally, because there are as yet only very few indications as to where these connections might lie. Because this is now so hard to do, people tend to acquire information by "hearing about it" rather than "seeing it for themselves." Although this hearing about things often occurs while watching television, the overlay between the heard words and the selected image encourages the viewer to accept the report as it is given. The recent coverage of the Persian Gulf war in the media will illustrate this in a frightening way. Before the dependence of television and film image, one compensation for the authoritative program of the written text was the opportunity to do the visualizing for ourselves. DiPalma's work takes the loss of this compensation as a given. He then discovers that a truly improvisatory situation can arise internally as an artifact of the direct confrontation between language and sensory experience. There the everyday distinction between the representation of experience and experience itself breaks down. In such a universe language reverts to its primary components and functions — it tends to see function as playful interaction — handling replaces labelling, instead of literal exchange we have jumps and juttings, neither song nor speech what is seen and heard is a kind of scratching and wailing across the bands. It happens instantaneously and across time, but so quickly as to obscure the distinction between the concrete detail and the indication of duration.

WRITING AND PERSEVERING

1. *Debussy Letters*, selected and ed. Francois Lesure and Roger Nichols, trans. Roger Nichols (Cambridge: Harvard University Press, 1987), p. 122 (in a letter to Raoul Bardac, Saturday, 31 August, 1901).

2. ibid., p. 65 (in a letter to Ernest Chausson, Monday, 5 February 1894).

OTHER ROOF BOOKS

Andrews, Bruce. **Getting Ready To Have Been Frightened**. 116p. $7.50.

Andrews, Bruce. **R & B.** 32p. $2.50.

*Andrews, Bruce. **Wobbling.** 96p. $5.

Bee, Susan [Laufer]. **The Occurrence of Tune**, text by Charles Bernstein. 9 plates, 24p.$6.

Benson, Steve. **Blue Book**. Copub. with The Figures. 250p. $12.50

*Bernstein, Charles. **Controlling Interests**. 88p. $6.

Bernstein, Charles. **Islets/Irritations**. 112 pp. $9.95.

Bernstein, Charles (editor). **The Politics of Poetic Form**. 246p. $12.95.

Brossard, Nicole. **Picture Theory**. 188p.$11.95.

Child, Abigail. **From Solids**. 30p. $3.

Davies, Alan. **Active 24 Hours**. 100p.$5.

Davies, Alan. **Signage**. 184p.$11.

Day, Jean. **A Young Recruit**. 58p. $6.

Dickenson, George-Therese. **Transducing**. 175p. $7.50.

Di Palma, Ray. **Raik**. 100p.$9.95.

Dreyer, Lynne. **The White Museum**. 80p. $6.

Edwards, Ken. **Good Science**. 80p. $9.95.

Eigner, Larry. **Areas Lights Heights**. 182p. $12, $22 (cloth).

Gizzi, Michael. **Continental Harmonies**. 92p. $8.95.

Gottlieb, Michael. **Ninety-Six Tears**. 88p. $5.

Grenier, Robert. **A Day at the Beach**. 80p. $6.

Hills, Henry. **Making Money**. 72p. $7.50. VHS videotape $24.95.
   Book & tape $29.95.

Inman, P. **Red Shift**. 64p. $6.

Lazer, Hank. **Doublespace**. 192 p. $12.

Legend. Collaboration by Andrews, Bernstein, DiPalma, McCaffery, and Silliman.
   Copub. with L=A=N=G=U=A=G=E. 250p. $12.

Mac Low, Jackson. **Representative Works: 1938-1985**. 360p. $12.95, $18.95 (cloth).

Mac Low, Jackson. **Twenties**. 112p. $8.95.

McCaffery, Steve. **North of Intention**. 240p. $12.95.

Moriarty, Laura. **Rondeaux**. 107p. $8.

Neilson, Melanie. **Civil Noir**. 96 p. $8.95.

Pearson, Ted. **Planetary Gear**. 72 p. $8.95.

Perelman, Bob. **Face Value**. 72p. $6.

Robinson, Kit. **Ice Cubes**. 96p. $6.

Seaton, Peter. **The Son Master**. 64p. $4.

*Sherry, James. **Part Songs**. 28p. $10.

Sherry, James. **Popular Fiction**. 84p. $6.

Silliman, Ron. **The Age of Huts**. 150p. $10.

Silliman, Ron. **The New Sentence**. 200p. $10.

Templeton, Fiona. **YOU-The City**. 150p. $11.95.

Ward, Diane. Facsimile (Photocopy of **On Duke Ellington's Birthday,
   Trop-I- Dom, The Light American**, and **Theory of Emotion**). 50p. $5.

*Ward, Diane. **Never Without One**. 72p. $5.

Ward, Diane. **Relation**. 64p. $7.50.

Watten, Barrett. **Progress**. 122p. $7.50.

Weiner, Hannah. **Little Books/Indians**. 92p. $4.

*Out of Print

For ordering or complete catalog write:
SEGUE DISTRIBUTING, 303 East 8th Street, New York, NY 10009